BREATHING
Hope

Bruce T. Anderson

ISBN 978-1-64559-170-2 (Paperback)
ISBN 978-1-64559-171-9 (Digital)

Covenant Books, Inc.
11661 Hwy 707
Murrells Inlet, SC 29576
www.covenantbooks.com

Dedicated to Kit and Dan

CONTENTS

FOREWORD

My name is not Allie. I am a breather of hope!

The story of "Allie and the Mystery of the Floating Boots" in chapter three tells my story. When I read it, I smiled. I remembered I didn't smile much when it happened. You will have to read it to better understand. I even laughed out loud when I remembered the airport security adventure. Hiking in the dark and hoping the bears were sleeping was no smiling matter at the time. It certainly is now.

But experiencing the quiet of the morning sky as the sun rose over that mountain, I didn't smile or laugh. As I read the words of my story, I remembered the moment and cried. Standing on that mountaintop was one of the most genuine and peaceful moments of my life. I closed my eyes to take it all in. When I did, I heard the whisper… If I can accomplish this, what else can I accomplish that I have never dreamed possible?

"Allie's" story is true.

To be honest, I really don't remember when the abuse started in my life. It was always there as long as I can remember. It was severe. The hopelessness from the daily physical and mental pain had become normal for me. I was broken beyond repair and valueless.

I do remember the day when good started happening, I didn't recognize it at the time. It was a cold Friday in early January to be exact. It was late, and the sun was setting on the snowy countryside. My social worker had taken me for admission into yet another program. I had been in many.

I still remember the numb feeling, like it was just another place to be bounced. At the time, I didn't know this, but the admissions staff didn't want to accept me. My problems were too great. My social worker was almost in tears when she said she didn't know where I would go for the night. I felt hopeless. Then a man came and met with me. It seemed we talked for a long time. When we finished talking, I was invited to see my new room and meet the other girls. I learned later that he was Mr. Anderson. He was the director of San Mar at the time and is the author of this very book. I didn't know it then, but he was a breather of hope, and that night I had started to breathe for the first time.

Many talks would follow. I don't remember everything we talked about, but I remember he always took the time to listen to me. He always had faith in me even when I didn't. He always hoped in me, when I didn't have hope in myself or even in life. It was at San Mar where I actually started to open up and share my whole story. It was at San Mar where I knew I was safe. I was respected. I was a human, and I had genuine value. I was on a path that had a future. I didn't see it then. It actually took me a while to see it. (Years to be honest.) I didn't know it, but breathing hope was life-changing, and I would never be the same.

I hope you enjoy this book and these true stories, and I hope you too breathe hope deeply.

Allie

PREFACE

Since the early seventies I have worked with youth. Most of those years have been devoted specifically to adolescents in residential care. For thirty-three of those years I had the privilege to serve as the CEO of an organization that operated multiple group homes for adolescent girls. In addition we had a program of treatment foster care for boys and girls of all ages, an on campus school, an outpatient mental health clinic for the community and a transitional living program for older teen girls. There were other programs, but you get the picture. It was never boring.

I learned very early that each of the children and youth we served faced their own unique challenges. Too often those challenges had left deep emotional scars formed through multiple traumas they had experienced over time. To many of them, those experiences had been overwhelming, robbing them of all vision and hope of a future. It became evident very quickly that hopelessness often had a first name:

- Hallie lived locked in a closet with only a bucket. She didn't go to school. She couldn't. She was let out only to please the men her parents brought to her. She had no friends. No one could know the many secrets she held.
- Jill's father beat her until she miscarried. Then he sent her to school. The note simply said, "Why do you make me do this?" His body was found in her bedroom still holding the shotgun. Both Jill and her miscarried baby were his girls.
- Rene's mother murdered her two older sisters and kept their small bodies in the freezer. Rene never understood why she was spared. Some questions are never asked out

loud. Two years later, she escaped through an upstairs window. She was found walking in her underwear in the dark of the early morning. She was six.

- Dawn remembered being hung up on a coat rack as a young child and touched by her mother's boyfriends in ways that hurt beyond words. She doesn't remember when the nightmares began.

- Brenda's mother dropped her off at the mall one morning with her baby sister. Mall security found her that night waiting on a bench after closing holding her crying sister. Her mother never returned. Brenda was five that day. She never understood.

- Marla told what was happening. She spoke truth. No one believed her. She was just a kid, and he was a successful businessman. His house burned to the ground. The abuse ended.

Each had seen things no child should see. Each held secrets they knew not to expose. Each knew never to trust. None could define trauma, but each knew it intimately. To each, the shadows of hopelessness had become familiar. But…each would be sent to us. Each would come to breathe hope deeply, and their worlds would change forever.

Even lacking vision, many of the hundreds who came to us nonetheless, unofficially declared themselves to be on a journey to independence where they were certain they would find happiness waiting at the gates when they arrived. Happiness seemed to be a common destination, but all too often, it was a journey for which they had no map or plan. Such thoughts were typically intimidating and scary yet often holding them captive and producing memorable behaviors as they struggled with the competing emotions of terror and excitement at the prospect of stepping into adulthood, often alone and without family support. Over the years, experience taught me that the most powerful action I could accomplish in my position at the top of the organization's food chain was to acknowledge the God-Given value in a youth by looking them in the eyes and listening intently to what they were, and often weren't, trying to say. Over time, this practice of listening opened doors with many who had determined never to trust. It was rarely a fast process. Someone compared the change process in a teen to watching grass grow. Based on the frequency with which I have found myself sitting on my mower, I suspect grass grows faster. At times, I would ask if I could share my observations as to what was going on in the life of a particular youth. I knew that an invitation to share my honest observations regarding the struggles they were experiencing and the decisions they were making was in itself an indication that they were beginning to unlock their doors of trust. Eventually, I recognized that I had been given the opportunity to impact the entire environment through the practice of intentionally and consistently breathing hope…that is, genuinely valuing each individual and speaking truth in a manner that could be heard and could foster healing.

What follows are some of the lessons learned along the way that have shaped me and many others and given clarity as to the route toward a full and productive life. The names of the girls in each of the stories are not their actual names. The stories are real. The names have been changed to respect the girls whose stories are being told.

INTRODUCTION

The Road to Independence

In early September 2001, I flew out to Denver, Colorado, to complete the process of becoming a clinical responder to the families of victims of airline disasters. It was one week before such disasters were to change the world. My wife accompanied me, and when I completed my studies, we rented a car and headed up to Estes Park where we entered Rocky Mountain National Park and drove over Trail Ridge Road. I had learned that at 12,183 feet, it was the highest road in the continental United States that a car could be driven over. It was also said to be breathtakingly beautiful. We hoped to see for ourselves. As we entered the park and began the twenty-five-mile ascent, we passed a lone cyclist on a slow motion journey. Was he going to the summit? He appeared motionless as we sped past. Was such a feat even possible in the thinning atmosphere? I wondered. When we reached the restaurant and gift shop at the top, we pulled into the parking area and walked to the nearby overlook. We were above the tree line. It was early fall, yet snow still covered the ground. I was amazed how the lack of oxygen forced me to continually submit to periods of rest.

My mind wandered back to the anonymous cyclist so many miles ago. Had he given up and returned to Estes Park? Could he really do it? I had ridden a bicycle for many years but had never considered anything as challenging as the Rocky Mountains. Could it be done? The question pursued me.

Over the next three years, the thought of riding over the Rockies continued to haunt me as I would remember that lone cyclist. I had determined that such a challenge was indeed possible. In fact, I had come to learn that numerous persons had completed it successfully many times. It had, however, never been done by me. Whether or not it was possible for me remained to be seen. I intended to find out.

Aspen, Colorado, sits at an elevation of 7,908 feet above sea level and eight miles from the resort town of Snowmass. In late June of 2004, I flew into the small airport at Aspen and took a shuttle over to a hotel in Snowmass, where I had shipped my bike. I was finally going to take on the challenge of riding over three of the highest mountain passes in the nation. It was an organized event that drew over one thousand experienced cyclists from all across America for seven days of riding over four hundred challenging miles in the Rockies. By arriving four days early, I hoped to adjust to the thin air and thus avoid the altitude sickness that had been known to affect those not used to exercising so strenuously at such heights.

The night prior to the ride, I left the hotel and joined the others camping near the starting point of the week-long adventure. We would begin in Snowmass and follow the route laid out. Eventually, we would climb over 32,000 feet and cross three mountain passes, two of which were almost 13,000 feet high. That was the plan anyway. On the morning of the ride, I was awakened as the silence was broken by the sound of bikes leaving camp. It was still dark. There were no voices, only the sounds of tires on asphalt and gears shifting. I lay invisible inside a tent in a sea of tents that would soon evaporate as the sun slowly appeared. I thought about the day and what lay ahead. Mentally, I couldn't see past the mountain in the distance, but at the time, I didn't even realize it. In reality, the actual mountain wasn't yet visible from the camp, but it loomed large in my mind.

I wondered if I would be able to breathe above 10,000 feet while exercising so strenuously. The somewhat hilly eight-mile ride from Snowmass proved to be a warm up. In contrast to what was to come, it was fairly level riding over to Aspen. There were expensive bikes everywhere. Excitement was high. Adrenaline was flowing! Route 82 begins to gain in elevation immediately out of Aspen. It is gradual at first but relentless and continues on for the next twenty-four miles until reaching Independence Pass at 12,095 feet. It was still early when I passed through Aspen. The town was quiet. Traffic was light. It was a clear sunny day. The air was cool and about to get even cooler as the elevation increased. Would I be able to breathe over 10,000 feet? I didn't know. The mental battle was as challenging as the physical one. I had heard the horror stories of athletes suffering from altitude sickness. Hopefully, I had had time to adjust. Several miles past Aspen, someone had spray-painted the road: *The Climbing Starts Here.* I thought I had been climbing. By comparison to what was to come, I was to learn; I had not. That was only one of the many lessons that lay waiting for me.

Since committing to the ride during the previous winter, I had trained harder than I had ever trained. Now, the altimeter on my bike continually reminded me of the ever-thinning air. It was intimidating. It was magnetic. I was drawn! I was determined to go to the top or fall over trying.

Stroke after stroke, I pushed one pedal in front of the other, one breath at a time. I was moving forward. A car passed, and I wondered if I appeared motionless to them. Frozen in place, I remembered the lone rider three years earlier on his journey up Trail Ridge Road. What had inspired him to make that journey? As I climbed higher, I could see a valley spread out for miles below me. It was spectacular. I was still breathing. I enjoyed the moment and kept pushing one pedal in front of the other.

Another bend revealed a rushing waterfall on my left. To my immediate right was a cliff with a steep drop-off and a spectacular view.

Beauty surrounded me everywhere. The peak of the mountain seemed so distant, yet overwhelming even so far away. I focused on the boulders to my left. They were enormous. How had they gotten there? Did the snow cover them in the winter? Focus... Breathe... Push. Focus... Breathe... Push. Focus... Breathe... Push.

Still further on, I passed an abandoned cabin that had refused to collapse. Who were they who had chosen to come here and build that home? Had life been hard for them? Had they come looking for gold, or was it something else that brought them? What was their life like? I wondered as my focus shifted to the road in front of me. How much easier my life must be than theirs had been. It didn't feel like it at the moment. Focus... Breathe... Push. Focus... Breathe... Push. Focus... Breathe... Push.

I was above the tree line. It was hard, but clearly, I was breathing above 10,000 feet. The mountain peak, now easily visible, still loomed up ahead and taunted me. I pushed one pedal after the other. Breathing was becoming more and more difficult, but I was still conscious and moving forward. I was going to the top! Two hours later, I saw the sign announcing the summit. The air was cold. At that altitude, snow lay on the ground, but there was no question about it. I had succeeded. It was possible after all! The rest of the week lay in front of me. There was still over 20,000 feet of climbing in the week ahead, but the questions were gone. I was breathing at the top!

Then standing there at the top, I heard the silent whisper, "What else could you do that you never dreamed possible?" It was only then I realized that since leaving Snowmass hours earlier, I hadn't thought of anything but the distant summit that silently taunted me. I had not envisioned what it would be like racing down the other side of the mountain or even riding the remaining forty miles past the summit that day. I had not envisioned the rest of the week or anything I had to do after returning home. I had no vision as to what lay ahead. Later as I reflected on what I had accomplished, I realized that arriving at the summit was like walking out of a thick fog into a bright light. From Independence Pass, I could see forever. Well, not really, the actual view from the rest area was not all that revealing. However, it was in that light that I also realized that it really wasn't about standing at the summit, as exciting as it was; it was about the journey itself and the lessons gained along the way. It was the process of stepping outside the comfortable in a way that made me stronger on the inside. It was the destination that drew me, but the journey that was transforming me.

As I slowly moved toward the summit, I remembered arriving at a point of seeing it in the distance and knowing that I was going to stand there. I had clarity of vision that I would succeed at reaching the top, but I remained blind to the reality that the journey, as difficult as it was for me, was actually making me stronger in more than physical ways.

At that moment, the similarities of my journey to the struggles of many of the youth I had come to know over the years remained hidden from me. I was caught up in myself and didn't even know it.

However, as time passed and I managed to get a better grasp on the obvious, I realized that a remaining challenge was to be found in relating the truths of my journey to Independence Pass to the youth who were on their own journey to independence and the adults who cared about them deeply.

What follows are some of the stories and insight that grew out of this greater journey as, together with my staff, we learned to breath hope into the lives of the hopeless.

PART 1

The Journey

When we least expect it, life sets us a challenge to test our courage and willingness to change; at such a moment, there is no point in pretending nothing has happened or in saying that we are not yet ready. The challenge will not wait. Life does not look back.
—Paulo Coelho

No Looking Back

For thirty-three years and one month, I served as the CEO of San Mar Children's Home in Boonsboro, Maryland. The home founded in 1883 as the Washington County Orphanage, had provided care for almost a thousand children and youth before my arrival in 1985. By that time, the orphanage in America was becoming a distant memory. Few had seen it go. In its place, group homes had filled the void where children often spent years in residence with overall caring staff and limited resources.

Some were adopted or moved into foster homes. Some actually returned to their families. Then in 1980, the Adoption Assistance and Child Welfare Act or Public law 96–272 was enacted by congress. It was an act intended to respond to the concern that children were being removed from their families and placed into group care where they often remained for long periods of time without appropriate services. It hoped to promote safety, permanence, and well-being by moving children out of institutions and into foster homes quickly.

Additionally, the law established a continuum of care for out of home placements and mandated specific services for those in residential care. Another goal of the act was to encourage work toward reunification of the family and to avoid long-term foster care whenever possible. If the child could not be returned to the family, another plan was to be identified, placement with relatives, adoption, or some other resolution. In essence, it dealt the final blow to the American orphanage. The act also directed federal funds to those states demonstrating compliance.

In early 1983, monitors from Maryland's Social Services Administration conducted a review as part of the process to renew the organization's license to provide residential care. Unlike previous reviews, the recently enacted standards of the act were being held up as the new measure, lest the state should lose the federal funding made available through the act. At the time, only a few of those providing residential care across the nation seemed to be paying close attention to the connection between a law dealing with adoption and youth in group care.

San Mar was no exception. As a result, half of the youth in the group home were found to not be in the least restrictive placement, as the new law required, and were removed and placed in foster homes, returned to their families, or emancipated to live on their own. San Mar was given mandates to add a clinical director, which was another requirement of the law, and to admit youth with more challenging behaviors who would in turn be in placement for much shorter periods of time. Failure to respond would result in a halt being made to any further admissions to the program. Needless to say the board took the directives quite seriously. A new era had begun. At that time, the organization operated one group home. It was into this historic period of transition that I stepped into the role of CEO.

Nationally, the child welfare and juvenile justice systems were rapidly and forcefully moving away from the traditional group home model to one more behaviorally and clinically oriented. Our journey would eventually take us on a path to specialize in serving adolescent girls. We would see five additional group homes added, a school, an outpatient mental health clinic, a program of treatment foster care for girls and boys of all ages, and a program working directly with families in the community so as to prevent them from losing their children in the first place.

With the changes mandated by the act, firmly in place, a youth entering the program for the first time needed to have presenting issues that required the structure of the residential milieu as a prerequisite to gaining admission to a group home. Detailed treatment plans with measurable goals outlining services to be provided by clinical social workers and even psychiatrists had to be developed. We began to see kids coming to us with deeper emotional wounds than at any time previously.

> It was clear that efforts to control acting out behaviors often resulted in stability and were necessary to maintain a safe environment, but it was the healthy connections the girls formed that produced lasting change.

Sometimes the behaviors flowing from these wounds were loud and angry, but just as often, they were quiet and withdrawn. Most kids had a difficult time seeing beyond their present situation. There was no realistic understanding of a future. They couldn't see past the mountain of their own hurt. As a result, risk taking and acting out behaviors were common and often had been a factor in their removal from their homes. Carol was a great example.

At thirteen years old and less than five feet in stature, Carol could barely see over a steering wheel, not that she would have a need to sit behind one. Yet when she arrived at San Mar, it was with a charge of grand theft auto. It simply had to be an error.

It was not, or so her probation officer assured us. She had been picked up by the police when a patrol car pulled up next to her at a stop light. When the officer casually glanced over and saw what initially appeared to be a driverless car sitting at the light with the motor running, he did a closer look and saw a diminutive young girl barely peering over the steering wheel.

She was arrested and quickly sent to a state detention center for girls. It was not her first arrest. Eventually, she was transferred to us. As she formed relationships with our staff, her story began to emerge. As a very young girl, she had been molested by a much older cousin over a period of several years. She had been threatened not to tell or bad things would happen. Instead, she acted out in school and the community. Bad things were already happening.

Later, a "girlfriend" from school invited her to go along to visit an old man who lived in the neighborhood. The girlfriend explained that if they went to his house on the days he got paid that he would give them money. That was true, but he had also paid the girlfriend to bring young girls to him for his pleasure. Carol was one of those girls.

After paying her for what he forcibly did to her, he invited them both to come back again in two weeks when he would have some more money. He believed that giving her money for what he did made everything all right. Her cousin had taught her previously not to refuse.

Carol hadn't refused, but everything was not all right. Filled with a quiet rage, she determined to return, but for revenge, and not money. When he arrived home from shopping and began carrying the groceries into the house, she seized the opportunity handed to her. With the keys still in the car, she simply drove away. She had planned to wreck it, but the police intervened at the stoplight. She knew that no one would believe her story. Barely a teenager and already in trouble, she kept her secrets and remained silent.[1] Carol was only one of a

---

[1] This was reported to Child Protective Services. By that time others had also reported him and he was subsequently tried and found guilty of molesting multiple children. Her cousin had also been found guilty.

long line of young girls with deep trauma and too many secrets. At that time, there was little understanding of trauma informed care and limited research on the brain and adolescent behaviors, yet the line of kids who had known deep trauma coming to us in search of safety and healing was growing longer.

Over time, I observed that whereas my clinical social workers and psychiatrist were helping the girls move beyond what they had experienced, it was when staff members were able to form trusting connections with the girls themselves that change began to be evident that lasted beyond the boundaries and structure of the group home and followed them into life. It was clear that efforts to control acting out behaviors often resulted in stability and were necessary to maintain a safe environment, but it was the healthy connections the girls formed with caring adults who genuinely valued them that produced lasting change.

In 2001, the YMCA of America was deeply concerned with the problems they saw in the youth frequenting their facilities across America. Aggression, depression, violence, drugs, and family dysfunction appeared to be omnipresent. There seemed to be a deterioration in values everywhere. With ever increasing frequency, staff time was being consumed addressing the needs of those children with the most severe behaviors. Even though those acting out were in the minority, their behaviors were holding a majority of staff time hostage and impacting the entire environment. To understand what was happening and what action they should pursue as a national organization, they commissioned a study from the Dartmouth Medical School and Harvard University. That study, published in 2003 under the name "*Hardwired to Connect*,"[2] concluded that the brain functioned in such a manner that connections with other people were meant to be the norm. In fact, the researchers surmised, when healthy connections did not occur, the brain did not produce the proper chemicals

---

[2] Hardwired to Connect: The New Scientific Case for Authoritative Communities, Commission on Children at Risk, Institute for American Values, 2003.

for stable living. This in turn resulted in problems with youth being unable to form healthy attachments, resulting in social dysfunction exactly like the YMCA was seeing. It directly supported the conclusions that we are social beings with a need to learn how to form and maintain healthy relationships. If we are to experience genuine fullness to life in our journey, we must develop and maintain those healthy relationships or connections.

The study went on to conclude that there needs to be a framework, which creates a balance between an appropriate structure in a youth's life that defines realistic and safe boundaries, and healthy nurture that validates the individual's inherent value.

Such balance is then maintained and strengthened through personal connections. These connections are formed through numerous points of contact or opportunities that demonstrate value and encourage responsible decision-making and personal ownership.

I used to believe that I couldn't change another person, but I could create an environment in which others would want to change and grow. The Hardwired to Connect research indicated that I could, in reality, change the brain structure of another person as I repeatedly valued them in healthy ways.

I began to look at how connections with youth, who had known trauma, were formed. I realized we had to first look to our own belief systems. I have come to realize that what a person believes is very important. It shapes who they are and drives what they do. Actually, I have come to understand that a person's beliefs are not always revealed by what they say. A person's true beliefs are revealed by their actions. Therefore, for me, to truly understand what a person believes, I need to listen intently to what they say and watch closely what they do.

I began with the presupposition that each individual is created in the image of God and subsequently has inherent worth. I was fully aware that I lived daily in a world that tended to agree with the concept of inherent worth, but at the same time acted as if personal worth was only realized when certain measures were obtained. Such measures might include having the right friends, having the right degrees, attending the right school, making enough money, and living in the right neighborhood. The list goes on and on and is always specific to the individual. I also realized that the girls being sent to us had typically been told the opposite, that is, they did not have value (and probably never would). Subsequently, they tended to act like it.

I needed to take the initiative to value each girl in the program. Furthermore, I needed to surround myself with a team of adults, who also recognized inherent value in each person. If one adult, forming a healthy connection with a youth, could positively change brain structure, what would happen if an entire team of genuinely caring adults linked arms (so to speak) and together resolved to love and value the youth in care?

The prospects were exciting. I began looking for ways to form these connections. It was important that we, as a team, define our belief system and have a clear understanding as to what the youth we were serving actually believed.

ANYA AND THE ROAD
TO NOWHERE

When a girl with challenging behaviors runs away to help her siblings, she fails because she ran in the wrong direction. But was it really a failure?

I'm not sure if it was really late at night or really early in the morning when the call came. The police had just picked Anya up and were returning her. She was frantic and on the verge of losing complete control. They wanted me to be present when they arrived.

When the patrol car pulled in the drive, she was sitting in the back. The handcuffs seemed to control her aggression but had no effect at all in stopping the profanities and threats that flowed from her mouth.

Anya couldn't remember how old she was when her father abandoned the family. Actually, she couldn't remember much about him at all. What she did remember was raising her four siblings.

As an alcoholic, her mother seemed incapable of even taking care of herself. Anya did what was needed. She always had. She promised herself that her brothers and sister would be safe even if she hadn't always been. It was a promise she had worked hard at keeping.

Eventually, when a perceptive teacher began questioning the bruises that she had worn to school, an investigation followed. Anya and her siblings were taken out of the home and placed in a series of group homes. For reasons, she didn't understand. She was never placed in the same group home as her siblings. Unable to keep her promise, she continually feared for their safety, but she would not reveal the secrets that only the family knew. As a result, she seemed to live in a near constant state of anxiety that was seldom understood by those around her.

Word came to her, delivered by her social worker, that her mother had entered a rehabilitation program in an effort to have her kids returned to her. At least, that's how it was explained to Anya. The anxiety in her didn't ease. She had seen this act before and really didn't believe it.

To demonstrate her commitment to her kids, or maybe just to ease the humiliation of having the state prying into her affairs, Anya's mother relocated to Hagerstown after successfully completing her treatment program. She was now only ten miles from Anya and in proximity to demonstrate her new dedication to motherhood.

Several months later, Anya was not surprised that her mother had not contacted her. She understood. What she did not understand was why her brothers and sister had been returned to her mother's new home. Anya had been the parent, and she feared for the safety of her family. Her anxiety could no longer be contained.

Her plan was to go to her mother's home. She ran alone. It was late at night, and the roads were empty. When she found a bicycle in a nearby yard, she took it. Seven miles later, the tires were flat. She abandoned it along the side of the road and continued on foot. A short time later, the police found her walking along the same road. She was trying to get to her mother's home but traveling the entire time in the wrong direction. When the police asked her where she was going, she told them, "Nowhere." It was truer than she knew.

After speaking with one of the officers outside for a few moments, I walked in the front door and was greeted with a cacophony of shouting. It was coming from Anya and an equally distraught police officer. Surrounding them were several other police officers and two staff, none of whom seemed to be celebrating her return at the moment. As I approached, I noticed the plastic cuffs she was wearing.

In many ways, Anya was very much like everyone else. She had a need to be treated with respect. It is a big deal, especially when absent. I realized that Anya, like most youth today, held a belief that respect is reciprocal. That is to say, as long as a person treated her with respect, she felt obligated to treat them somewhat respectfully or at least, not disrespectfully.

However, if a person were to behave toward her in a disrespectful manner, the rules all changed. She would no longer be under any obligation whatsoever to show them respect in return. All respect is viewed as conditional and circumstantial. I recognized the police officer standing in front of her at the moment had been placed into that category.

Reciprocal respect feels right. We respect those who are worthy based upon their demonstrated behaviors. We have heard the expression; "If you want respect, you will get it just as soon as you start showing some!" It just makes sense! Or does it? Growing up, Anya had never known respect at home. It was unrealistic to expect her to initiate such attitudes and behaviors under stress when the reality of respect was foreign to her. We could just as easily expect her to speak to us in fluent Swahili. It simply wasn't going to happen.

When I approached Anya, she was still screaming obscenities. I stood directly in front of her and very quietly asked her if it was all right to remove the cuffs. She kept yelling at the one officer with whom she was particularly upset. I stood between the two of them and looked her directly in the eyes. Again, almost in a whisper, I asked, "Anya, why are you disrespecting me like this? Have I ever disrespected you?"

If someone would have slapped her in the face, it could not have had a more dramatic impact on her. In an instant, she stopped and looked at me; the rage she had flaunted put on hold. Clearly, she was processing what I had said to her. Had she disrespected me? She knew how painful it was to be disrespected. Hesitantly, she explained, "I wasn't talking to you." Then much louder, "I was talking to him." She looked directly at the officer. Certainly, that made it okay. I realized everything she knew about healthy respect was what we had demonstrated to her in the short time she had been with us.

"Anya," I slowly spoke her name. Using a person's name in a calm manner in the midst of a crisis can help to de-escalate a situation. "I don't like seeing you in these cuffs. Are you able to control yourself so that we can remove them?" Probably a pretty good idea at the moment.

I realized that removing the cuffs at that moment might not be wise. I suspected if the police maintained a list of "Outstanding Ideas from Leading Citizens," removing her cuffs was probably not going to be on it. However, I could see her regaining control of her emotions as we spoke.

"Just tell him ..." Still angry and more of a growl than a bark, but quiet enough that only I could hear.

"Anya, I'm talking to you. Are you able to take control of yourself so we can take these off of you?"

She became quiet and then mumbled to me, "Yes...You can take them off."

The officers weren't quite convinced but complied when I asked for them to be removed. I lead Anya by the hand into the dining room and asked her to sit at a table while I went back and spoke with the officers.

If a youth has never known respect, isn't it understandable when she fails to act in a respectful manner at those times when I think she should? It is also true that if I apply her own belief to her (i.e. You get respect when you show respect.) it may be a long time, if ever, before I am obligated to show any respect toward her at all.

This is where the real problem appears to lie! A belief that grants respect when it has been earned and is based on the actions of the individual is like a pit of quicksand. Instead, we need to look beyond the obvious and see the person.

> ## If a youth has never known respect isn't it understandable when she fails to act in a respectful manner at those times when I think she should?

In the first chapter of the Bible, in the book of Genesis, we are told that God created the human race in his own image and declared it as being good![3]

If we can accept that as true, we realize that because we have been formed in the image of the creator himself, each person comes into the world with an inherent value to their being.

If a child grows up with unconditional nurture and support, he or she begins to realize over time the truth of their inherent value. She can then learn to act and dream accordingly. However, if nurture and support are absent or very conditional, and instead, there is scorn and trauma, a different set of actions and beliefs result.

If I presuppose that a person is created in the image of God and therefore has inherent value, then I must take the next step and choose to view that person as worthy of respect. Such a belief, and

---

[3] Genesis 1:27, 31

the subsequent action to respect another person (How powerful it is when respect becomes a verb!) is based not on the learned behaviors of the individual, which are often woefully lacking, but on the person they were created to be.

The problem is that typically before respect is granted there is first a focus on behavior. A person is deemed to be worthy of respect when they behave in the proper manner. That becomes quite confusing when different groups have differing standards as to what is acceptable for inclusion.

A teen's peers will often present standards different from the adults in their life. A youth may be deemed to have value when for example: others find them attractive and slim, or they get good grades, and are good athletes, or they do drugs, or they don't care about grades and are willing to stand in opposition to authority, and the list goes on and on. It all becomes subjective unless we accept the truth of being created in the image of an unchanging God. It is easy to see why so many youth struggle with their own self-worth when that worth is conditional and based on their ability to earn it on a daily basis according to changing standards.

Does the recognition that each individual has inherent worth and value suggest then that we should be accepting and tolerant of behaviors that are clearly inappropriate? Should we just overlook the negatives in an attempt to make up for the nurturing they may have missed in earlier years?

We could do that. However, to do so misses the point of the true value of the individual. If a person has value and worth, then it follows that their actions really do matter. Self is no longer the center of the universe. Accountability to others becomes important to help the individual grow from selfishness into selflessness, an important variable for living successfully in a society with others. However, such a move usually needs to be modeled to be grasped.

Correction of the individual youth (when accompanied by respect) helps them gain control of their own life as they are presented with opportunity to learn from their experience and grow from it.

Correction is the application of accountability that enables a youth to mature into a healthy adult. The role of the responsible adult is to provide the appropriate feedback and instruction so as to help them see how their behavior is hindering their growth toward becoming a productive adult. When the adult is in a position of authority, this may also include appropriate consequences.

It is also worth noting that correction is a concept unfamiliar to many of the youth coming to us. Punishment, on the other hand is quite familiar. It is focused on behaviors in the past and is typically linked to and often triggered by the emotions of the adult.

> Eventually her rage subsided. She had broken $400 worth of dishes as I stood by and watched.

Unlike correction, which may take time and flows from relationship, punishment can produce the immediate results of establishing control and a stable environment. It can also produce some very negative and long lasting effects in children and youth, such as: guilt, shame, bitterness, resentment, regret, self-pity, and fear.

In contrast, correction is relationship-based and future-focused, always pointing toward growth and hope. It has nothing to do with retribution and everything to do with personal ownership and forward motion. Whereas, punishment is often based on the feelings of the adult; the purpose of healthy discipline is for correction and growth with emotions not dictating outcomes. Retribution, shame, and guilt have no role. The motivation for correction is always for the good of the child. Correction always holds the child's best interests, not the adult's anger, in the forefront. It is never out of control.

As for Anya, she really was able to calm down that night and eventually went to bed. She never did return to her mother's home but managed to graduate from high school then went on to become a paramedic. After several years, she joined the military where she served as an army medic in Iraq. As of this writing, she has completed her army service, and after a relatively brief time as a civilian emergency medical technician, she enlisted in the marines where she is making a career while raising her daughter with her husband.

Before coming to San Mar, Anya had been in numerous group homes and foster homes. Her running away and acting out had made it difficult for any of them to maintain her in a way that she would be safe. The effect had been that she had come to believe that she was truly an unlovable kid who people viewed as hopeless and bad. The trauma of losing her father, rejection by her mother, the uncertainty of her siblings' safety, and numerous emotional scars she received from a long line of her mother's boyfriends had reinforced the message to her. It was never clear if her trauma made the attention deficit disorder, a label a psychiatrist had given to her several years earlier, worse or if they were two separate issues. It really didn't matter. Life was a challenge. The deep concern she had for her siblings was an indication that she was a genuinely caring person. It was a character trait later demonstrated repeatedly in her service as a medic. She needed help seeing past the hurt, and she needed understanding that she truly had value. She wasn't a bad person, but it was also evident that in trying to help her siblings, she wasn't a very good problem solver.

There were several runaway incidents in which Anya was returned late at night in handcuffs by the police. Each time she had run, she had feared for the safety of her siblings, who were living with their mother. Each time, she had run alone and in the wrong direction.

As we continued to wrestle with how we could most effectively respond to Anya, and the many others we were not able to serve, a commitment was made by the board to raise the funding necessary to construct a facility through which we could adequately meet the needs of the many Anyas in the larger child welfare system.

The result was the Jack E. Barr Therapeutic Group Home. It opened on August 2, 1997, and remained open daily until December 2, 2014, when the organization shifted to working with youth in the context of their own families. There were 232 girls who lived in the home during that time. Thanks to Anya who had been the inspiration for the development of such an intense program; many came to breathe hope and left the program far stronger than when they arrived.

Very quickly, we learned that most of the girls being admitted to the new program, like Anya, had extensive histories of deep hurt in their lives. It was recognized that too often severe acting out became the norm, so it was mandated that all staff in therapeutic group homes throughout the state who were working directly with youth had to be trained and certified in approved methods of restraining out of control youth in care.

We had even been advised to construct our new facility with a padded "quiet room" in it. The room had a one-way mirror, cameras for safety, and a big metal door with multiple locks. We were told that the level of disturbance of some of the girls was so severe that restraint training and locked quiet rooms were necessary realities.

It wasn't very long before we learned that there was a great deal of validity in what we had been told. We were finding that most of the girls coming to us already had extensive histories of having been restrained. The padded quiet room was very familiar to most.

By 2005, I had grown very uncomfortable with the staff having to restrain girls due to acting out behaviors. We had been told it was normal, and we had accepted that reality. As a result, it had become a part of our organizational culture. It seemed to me that the use of restraints maintained a safer environment but also a culture of control. For a girl with a history of abuse and trauma, such an intervention appeared to complicate the healing process.

I sat down and began to think about what I believed about working with kids. The result came to be known as our Culture of Care philosophy. I realized that there may be a time when restraining a kid with a history of abuse might be necessary to keep her, or others, safe. However, it should be the exception and never the norm.

We began to focus on personal responsibility as never before. It wasn't very long before a young girl, very accustomed to having her own way in everything, heard the word *no*. When she did, she began yelling at the staff and other kids. When that didn't convince anyone of the righteousness of her demands, she went into the kitchen and took a plate and smashed it on the floor.

It was at that point I arrived at the house. Staff were clearly ready to put a stop to her foolishness and were waiting for my signal. Instead, I asked them to stay with the other girls as I went into the kitchen and watched as the angry teen proceeded to smash every dish, plate, bowl, etc.

Eventually, her rage subsided, and one of the staff was able to sit with her and listen as she poured out her heart. As she did, another staff was able to inventory the damage. By the next morning, I had replaced everything. When I did, I met with her and explained to her what I was doing. I let her know that I believed she was a person of extreme worth. Therefore, what she did mattered. I wasn't angry with her, but I did need to replace the dishes as all the girls needed them. I was expecting her to pay the bill. It was $400. She explained to me that I was dreaming, and she wasn't about to pay. After all, we had not stopped her. In fact, she pointed out. I sat nearby and watched her as she broke them.

I explained how I understood and would certainly not force her to pay, but in order for her to remain in the program, which I very much wanted her to do, she had to demonstrate to me that she was indeed a responsible person. If she needed someone to restrain her because she was unable to control herself, it made me wonder if she was responsible enough to be here. If she was unable to accept responsibility for her actions, then she must be expecting someone else to be responsible for what she did. I explained to her that if it was her intention for me to pay for her broken dishes, then she was not ready to live in the house. I also explained that I realized she probably did not have $400, so I would give her things to do which would enable her to work off her debt.

It is an understatement to tell you that it was not quite what she was expecting.

She initially refused. However, after several days of eating off of paper plates, and being informed we were going to proceed with helping her find a more suitable program, she not only worked off the debt, we never had another broken dish nor did she throw another tantrum during her stay.

For almost three years, we went without any restraints whatsoever. Eventually, monitors from the Social Services Administration came and conducted an investigation. They were concerned that we were failing to report restraints, which was mandated. They interviewed all the residents and all the staff. They came to the conclusion; it wasn't happening.

I remember hearing several of the girls talking about being restrained in other programs. I was surprised to learn that each one of them knew exactly how many times they had been restrained and how many times they had been put into a padded quiet room.

One girl announced that she had been restrained forty-six times. I told her that I was quite surprised to hear that. She had never been restrained with us at all. I asked her how that was even possible. Without hesitation, she looked at me and, as if stating the obvious, explained, "Oh, you can't act like that here!"

Not long afterward, I was standing in the back hallway talking with two of the girls when one of our social workers came through with a mother and daughter. It was not uncommon for families to visit prior to placement of a girl in the program. I realized they were taking a tour to see if this was the place they wanted to trust with their daughter.

I noticed that the mother saw the quiet room as she walked by with its big metal door and multiple locks, and her eyes got quite big. The girl, however, didn't react to it at all. I realized the girl had been in placements before and had been in quiet rooms. She was familiar with restraint. I realized that whereas the mother had seen her daughter throw multiple tantrums in the past, she had never seen her placed in such a room.

By this point, we had not used the room at all for a very long time, so when they came past us again, I asked Allie, one of the girls I was talking with, to explain to the mother what the padded room was, that had the heavy door with the big locks.

Allie, without missing a beat, smiled and said, "Oh that's where they lock us all up!" It was meant to be humor, and Allie and the other girl I was talking with both laughed, but mom wasn't catching it.

"Allie, tell them the last time you ever saw the door shut, or someone actually in the room."

To which, she responded, "What do you mean?" Then she recognized the panicked look in mom's eyes and assured her, "Oh, it never gets used. I've never seen anyone in it or even the door shut."

I had the door removed the next day. We had new norms.

With this lesson in mind, we sought to provide youth in our care with a milieu, which provided a balance between appropriate structure (that which was understanding of, and responsive to, the unique needs of the youth) and healthy nurture (personal connection based on a recognition of genuine and inherent value). This balance between seemingly competing ends was delivered in the context of abundant opportunities so as to create multiple points of contact, resulting in life-changing connections.

It wasn't very long before Allie was invited to participate in one of the most life-changing opportunities of her entire life. When that time arrived, she was ready.

Allie and the Mystery of the Floating Boots

It was in processing my own experience of riding my bike over the Rockies that I resolved to find a summer camp in Colorado where I could send the girls so they could experience a similar opportunity for personal growth as I had known.

I planned to place them into what I was considering as "intentional disequilibrium." That is, I hoped to intentionally take the girls out of their comfort zones and place them in an environment totally foreign to them, where they were safe and supported, but off balance. I thought the natural tendency when thrown off balance in an unfamiliar environment would be to turn to the known and hold on tight. The known would be the staff accompanying them. It would be a nurturing environment but would stretch them and challenge them to grow.

Considering my experience in Colorado, it seemed to be a perfect location. Most of the girls in care had never flown or even been in an airport. The experience of flying to Colorado where they would be greeted by the Rocky Mountains as they landed in Denver was very appealing.

I had learned long ago that the script usually doesn't go the way I think it should. This was no exception. I had also learned that when I can take the time to provide an overview of what was about to happen, things tended to go much smoother. I had tried to do that,

41

however, I was to learn that my explanation of getting through airport security had not been detailed enough.

Although I was not flying to Colorado with the group of ten girls and three staff, I did drive them to the airport. At Dulles, I was permitted to accompany the group right up to the gate.

I had explained the process of emptying pockets and putting shoes, belts, and backpacks in the containers as they prepared to go through screening. However, I watched as the TSA agent looked at one of the girls, who was indeed ready to go through the metal detector and signaled for her to proceed. I instantly knew what was about to happen and felt powerless even as I shouted *"Stoooooop"* from where I stood only ten feet away.

What I saw happening didn't stop. As he signaled the girl who was ready, three others wearing their daypacks, filled to capacity, assumed he had just given clearance for the whole group to go through. Each one determined to be the first.

My instruction about, one at a time through the metal detector, seemed to have been forgotten.

I learned that day how to get the automatic doors that close off an entire wing at an international airport to actually move. Another interesting trivia fact is when those doors shut, the wing is evacuated. All of it! Well, I wanted the girls to be safe. Thankfully, a supervisor arrived on the scene with relative speed and quickly grasped what had happened before the evacuation had moved very far. Our entire group was wearing very colorful shirts that announced they were all on the "Adventure Team." I think more than a few people, TSA agents included, were hoping we were not there to create our own adventure in the airport. There is no question we were noticed. The girls seemed to be enjoying all the attention thoroughly. The adventure had certainly begun!

I had found a high adventure camp nestled in the mountains near Gunnison that welcomed the girls and the staff I sent to them. Initially, the camp director assured me that there was no need for our staff to attend. If they did, it would be at the same full cost of the camp as I had paid for each camper. I sent the staff.

It was during that week. One of the camp's counselors found that a very nice pair of hiking boots she owned had disappeared. They were later found floating (partially) in the sludge at the bottom of the camp's outhouse. Even professional cleaning wasn't going to rescue the once expensive boots. It was a mystery as to how they got there.

I spoke with my staff who were there at the camp in Colorado and realized a problem had escalated to a point where sending them back was a wise move.

Very shortly afterward, the camp director was on the phone to me "requesting" to have two of our ladies returned to us as soon as possible. Camp staff were willing to drive the two hours to the airport and pay the additional fees to change the tickets if we arranged to have someone meet the girls at Dulles. Actually, I am not really sure if someone meeting the girls was high on their agenda.

I spoke with my staff who were there at the camp and realized a problem had escalated to a point where sending them back was a wise move. I agreed to meet the girls.

The next day, I was there to meet them when they arrived. On the drive back, I stopped and bought them lunch. It afforded us the opportunity to talk about what had occurred.

They spoke over each other telling me about all the activities they had experienced. I could tell from the excitement that there had been a lot of positives. I pressed as to what had created the problems. They explained how they had gone on a long hike. I suspect from the way they had been talking that it started out being a hike they were happy to be doing. However, after hiking six difficult miles, the camp staff realized they had taken a totally wrong trail and had everyone turn around and go back.

When they finally arrived back at the van, they were exhausted and finished. It was at that point the camp staff pointed to a different trail and announced that was the right one, followed by, "Let's go."

My staff later reported that they, too, felt as if that had to be a bad joke. Everyone was totally worn out. One of the girls having lunch with me had requested something from the van. When the camp staff, with the nice boots, unlocked the door, both girls climbed in and refused to get out. Actually, it was more like they dared anyone to try and remove them. It became clear that removing them from the van was going to create some long time memories for everyone.

Eventually, the camp staff wisely rethought the schedule for the day and everyone got in the van and returned to the camp. However, the exhaustion in the two girls, combined with a long history of problem solving that was not always exemplary, led to a division between the girls and the camp staff that seemed to fester.

As we sat in the restaurant, they both laughed as they went on to describe how they had taken her fancy boots later that night and "floated" them in the outhouse. They laughed hard until the realization whom they had just told gradually washed over them.

Truthfully, there was some humor in how they masterfully related their crime. I did find myself chuckling, but when I stated, "They were $150 boots. How do you think we should deal with this?" The humor was an instant memory, and they both told me that what they did was wrong, and they should pay for the boots. I agreed with them. If you are a person of worth, then what you do matters. I was also proud of them for their willingness to accept responsibility and told them so. They ended up splitting the cost, and I sent the money directly to the counselor. The following year we went again to the same camp. That time, there was a requirement from the camp that my staff attend, and a significant discount was given to each along with a hearty welcome waiting for them.

Was the program worthwhile? It was not a budgeted item, so each year we had to raise the funding necessary to send the girls. It was encouraging to observe the visible impact that seemed to occur. Even the two girls who had returned early seemed to have grown through the experience. If you are going to intentionally throw a kid into a state of disequilibrium, then you need to be prepared to deal with all the side effects.

Due to an extensive history of trauma, Allie had always had a very difficult time envisioning any kind of future for herself. She particularly could not imagine herself living a healthy and fulfilling life. She believed she was broken beyond repair.

Upon returning, she told the story of how the group had hiked up a very challenging mountain. As they neared the top, it was getting late, so the guide directed them to an area where they would camp for the night. By the time their tents were up, it was already dark. The guide talked about how the next morning they would have the opportunity to get up while it was still dark and hike to the summit to watch the sun rise. She then went on to warn them that they needed to use caution if they got up during the night. There were bears in the area, and they should not be wandering away from the camp, nor were they to have any food in their tents.

Bears! Seriously?

The next morning as the guide went around to each tent, Allie was the only one who made the decision to risk leaving the apparent sanctuary of her tent and stepping into the dark for the journey to the top. Even all, but one, of the staff chose to sleep in that morning.

As Allie shared her experience, she remembered walking along in the dark, close to the guide, hoping bears slept late. It was evident as she spoke, that what was presented as humor had in reality been a demonstration of great courage. Then as she shared how she stood at the top as the sun appeared over the distant mountains, her voice cracked with emotion, and she paused.

> If you are going to intentionally throw a kid into a state of disequilibrium, then you need to be prepared to deal with all the side effects.

"As I watched the sun rise, I realized I had just done the impossible."

Again, she paused. "What else could I do that I never thought was possible?"

Listening to her speak, I remembered standing at the top of Independence Pass, and I felt her emotion. I understood what she meant. She had heard the same whisper I had heard at the top of Independence Pass. It was transforming.

Following her trip, she demonstrated a new confidence, which she described as being found on top of a mountain in Colorado. When she first came to us, we were told that due to her extensive traumas she would undoubtedly live her entire life in some type of group setting. However, due to the life changing connections she formed with our entire team, she went on to graduate from high school while still with us. She later moved back with her family.

Today, she admits that there were still some rough times when she left, but she never forgot the whisper on the mountain. She went on to graduate from college and demonstrated the ability to hold down a full-time job.

Years later, she maintains the progress that she showed upon returning from camp. She is a loving wife and mother of two beautiful girls who both know they are loved deeply, and she is living without support from any mental health system at all.

I sent girls to Colorado for three years. In 2010, there seemed to be a lot of competing demands and not enough girls with an interest in hiking at high altitude where bears live.

One year later, the summer camp experience was rekindled with girls going to an Adventure Camp in the Seneca region of West Virginia. They had a great experience and repeated it again many times. I did miss the airport experience (Parts of it anyway).

Allie was just one of many examples of youth whose lives were transformed when they were valued by an entire team of caring adults. However, we learned that sometimes the experiences that a girl brought with her from her past made her so distrustful of others that she tended to push them away and resist any attempts to form a meaningful connection. How could such a girl be reached? Cris was one such example.

CRIS AND THE POWER OF TRUST

In 2005, we were asked to consider operating a program of shelter care for adolescent girls in the care of the Department of Juvenile Services. The department had recently completed an extensive gap analysis to identify existing needs for youth in their care throughout the state. The analysis determined a short-term program of shelter care up to thirty days for adolescent girls in Western Maryland, who did not pose a threat to the community, was a very high priority.

I had been warned by directors of other agencies to stay away from operating just such a shelter as it was very hard to sustain. Since the state would pay for the daily care of a girl, we needed to have enough youth in residence to cover the basic expenses. With a shelter, the census tended to change daily. You never knew if you were going to have a low census or a high census, and yet you had to pay your staff to be present every day. You also had to pay electric bills and other costs, like insurance; no matter how many kids were in residence. Our board had unanimously decided against operating such a program. The risk for serious fiscal loss was too great.

Then we got a visit from the Secretary of Juvenile Services, Kenneth Montague. For two hours, Secretary Montague talked about how such a program was needed in Western Maryland for adolescent girls. But it was when he talked about two girls, in particular who'd been placed into the detention centers operated by the department that he had our attention.

In hindsight, he reasoned that the two girls really did not need the intense structure of the locked detention centers, but the department had no other options available. As a result, both of the young girls, in totally unrelated incidents, had committed suicide while being detained. The secretary felt strongly that both girls would still be alive had a shelter as he was proposing been available. It was certainly hard sell.

At the conclusion of his presentation, he left, and we spent much time discussing what we had heard. It was clear; our members felt strongly that if there were a need in our community and we had the expertise to effectively respond to it, we had a moral obligation to do so. Another vote was taken, and this time, it was unanimous again; however, this time it was a unanimous commitment to proceed with a new shelter. They were aware of the risk.

We were advised that the girls who would be staying at the shelter could be there from one day up to ninety days. Many of them had been in the system for a while and were pretty hardened. We should construct a facility with cinder-block walls, concrete floors, and heavy institutional furniture. They would destroy anything less durable. These tough girls needed to be taught a lesson; we were told.

We had been working with youth with challenging behaviors for a long time, and we felt we knew whom we were serving. We also believed people responded to their environment and to the manner in which they were treated. We had no intent on punishing or fostering a message that time with us was in any way a punishment. Therefore, the facility we designed, constructed, and subsequently operated was beautiful and welcoming. It is interesting to note that there was rarely any malicious damage done by the girls living there the entire time it was in operation.

A little over a year after the secretary's visit, we had raised over a million dollars and had constructed a beautiful new facility. By mid-summer, we opened and began to admit girls in the care of the Department of Juvenile Services. Unlike girls coming from other agencies who were often placed in care as the result of the actions of others, girls entering from the Department of Juvenile Services came to us as a result of their own choices. Often those choices had not been very good. They were there by court order and, as we were warned, were often quite hardened when they arrived, typically in shackles and handcuffs. Cris was no exception.

"How quickly can you get me moved to the large group home?" Cris cornered me as soon as I entered the door. She had been living in our shelter for the past thirty days.

"What's the hurry, Cris?"

She went on to explain that as a resident in the shelter, she was attending our on grounds school. However, she was going to be a registered nurse. She needed to be enrolled in the public school, and that wasn't going to happen until she moved to one of our other programs. She needed me to make it happen...fast!

I smiled. She was going to be a registered nurse. A sense of déjà vu passed over me. I had had this conversation many times before but never enough and never with her. She had begun to create a future. She was beginning to hope. It was an indication that trust was beginning to take root. I knew that trust, or distrust, was historical in nature. That is, it was formed from past experience. Negative experiences in the past tended to leave a person trapped in the present, but when trust forms roots, it creates a bridge to the future, and the buds of hope appear.

The natural enemies of trust are cynicism, self-centeredness, and indifference and reveal an individual who tends to expect more from others than they are willing to give.

Typically, kids entering care are so self-focused on their own dysfunction and reminded so often of the obstacles ahead that they have a difficult time seeing into the future. There is no hope because trust, the seeds of hope, have not been sown. Most damaging, but nearly invisible, is the loss of creativity and vision.

I reminded her of the day she arrived. When I entered the building, she was in the front hallway talking with two of the staff. The glare in her eyes, her stance, the clenched fists, she was ready for anything that could be thrown her way.

> The natural enemies of trust are cynicism, self-centeredness and indifference and reveal an individual who tends to expect more from others than they are willing to give.

I mentioned to her that my first impression was that she was high on drugs and ready for trouble. She hesitated for a moment as if trying to find the right words.

"I knew I was going to court. The judge had told me the last time that if I returned to his court again, he was going to lock me up. I knew I couldn't handle it. I went out and got high. The next day, the judge decided to send me to the shelter instead of locking me up. He was going to give me a chance. It didn't feel like a chance. I decided I was going to run away that night. No one would find me. When they brought me to the shelter, I knew there were going to be problems. I had been locked up. I knew you always ran into trouble when you arrived in a new place."

"What you weren't ready for," I offered, "was to be met at the door by two staff who were genuinely glad to see you."

"I wasn't." Tears rolled down her face. "It was as if they saw something in me right then that I had never seen. After a couple of weeks, I started to believe them. I started to see it too."

One of the greatest enemies of trust is what has come to be known as "cordial hypocrisy." That is, pretending to trust. Such lack of genuineness is recognized pretty quickly in an untrusting adolescent and produces a kind of toxicity that always corrodes relationships and feeds the adolescent belief that adults are not to be trusted...ever.

Healthy confidence is a by-product of trust. Cris had probably never heard of "cordial hypocrisy" but could recognize it when she was in its presence. It seemed obvious that she had prepared herself for rejection, and when it did not come, she was thrown off balance. Eventually, as she began trusting that the message she was hearing was genuine, she started to dream...Trust had a long way to go, but the seeds had been sown, and the cultivation of hope was beginning.

Then after several months she noticed that people around her were changing. Specifically, her stepfather who had not wanted her back in his home was now talking with her and inviting her home for weekends. She couldn't believe how much he had changed in such a short period of time. The same thing was happening with her siblings and friends. It was amazing. Everyone around her was changing!

Trust, by its very nature, is very dynamic and results in change. What is really amazing is how powerful it is when we change our expectations to develop and unleash the inherent value of the individual instead of trying to control what we have defined as their dysfunction.

Although trust is not power, it is through trust that we can acquire the greatest power, not power over others but something far more important—the power over ourselves and taking ownership of our lives. That in turn creates the possibility for each and all of us to realize our full potential together. It is difficult to truly understand the perspective of another when we lack vision and become self-centered in the present.

Erik Erikson was a German-American developmental psychologist and psychoanalyst known for his popular theory on psychological development of human beings. It was his belief that we learn to trust in infancy, as modeled by our mothers in particular. It is in infancy and early childhood, he contended, that we receive our orientation to the world. At that point in our lives, trust is unthinking and accepting.

As we grow our understanding of, and ability to, trust expands and is enhanced or undermined by our experiences with others. Erikson saw that process, when enhanced, as basic trust maturing into authentic trust. Such authentic trust, like basic trust, is formed within the family system then grows to focus on relationships rather than single transactions and outcomes.

When needs go unmet, the child naturally becomes distrustful. When abuse is introduced, an inordinate suspicion of others is the result. It was evidenced in the look Cris brought with her that day she arrived in shackles.

Erikson wrote, "Someday, maybe, there will exist a well-informed, well considered, and yet fervent public conviction that the most deadly of all possible sins is the mutilation of a child's spirit, for such mutilation undercuts the life principle of trust."[4]

The cost of such abuse to America is not easily measured or quantified. The reality is that most don't know how to respond to children who carry the weight of trauma with them and have not thought a great deal about it. The costs of such absence of familial trust is staggering. In 2004, one estimate put the cost of complying with federal rules and regulations alone in the United States—put in place

---

[4] Erik Erikson, quoted in Jonathan Kozol's Death At An Early Age, (1967)

essentially due to lack of trust—at $1.1 trillion, which is more than 10 percent of the gross domestic product.[5]

The encouraging news is that a culture of trust and hope is attainable. Change is possible. Joni was a demonstration of what could happen when trust is built, and hope is breathed.

5 Stephen Covey, Keynote address at Linkage's Eleventh Annual Best of Organization Development Summit in Chicago, IL, May 12–14, 2009.

THE JONI CONNECTION

Joni had been in numerous group homes and had been invited to leave all of them. It wasn't long after Joni arrived at San Mar that she made it evident that she was both very intelligent and very accomplished at pushing others away. She quickly alienated most of the staff. Yet Joni stands as an example of the life-changing power of healthy connection established through abundant opportunity.

I realize that may need a bit of explanation.

In 1883, the Washington County Orphan's Home was established in downtown Hagerstown, Maryland. For forty-four years, it provided care to 978 children. Then in 1927, it moved into a modern new facility about ten miles away in the rural community of San Mar and became known as the Home at San Mar or the San Mar Children's Home.

By 1980, federal and state laws were changing, forcing historic changes on the child welfare system. The orphanage in America was gone. In its place, group homes had arisen to fill the void. Now with increasing demands for accountability and acceptance of youth with greater clinical issues than ever before, many programs were having a struggle making the transition. It was into this cauldron I was hired to grow the organization.

When I began my journey as the CEO of San Mar, I purchased a new bicycle and began riding as a discipline to cope with the inevitable stress I would find working with kids familiar with trauma and crisis. I realized that it is normal for youth in unfamiliar situations to try and create the familiar so as to give them reference points to the known in their lives. To those who have come out of an environment of trauma, what they often created around them was chaos. Therefore, I needed to be proactive in creating both, disciplines for strength in my own life and a stable environment for the kids.

In 1992, the Hagerstown Exchange Club, a local service organization, had the idea to recruit some volunteers to ride bicycles from Ocean City, Maryland, to Hagerstown, in the Western part of the state as a fundraiser. The members would find sponsors who would pledge support for each mile the cyclists would travel. They asked one of their members, Curt Bachtell, if he would consider doing the ride and if he would find two others who would join him.

Curt had been riding extensively with Ron Crist and myself as a result of friendships formed over the years. Together, the three of us would do the ride while the club covered all our expenses. To us, it seemed like a pretty good deal. To them, it seemed pretty amazing we would attempt such an endeavor. I thought it wise not to challenge their thinking.

By all accounts, it was a successful event ending with a picnic in Hagerstown's City Park as we came riding in. However, the following year, someone else was in charge of fundraising for the club, and they moved on to another idea.

With the Exchange Club no longer interested, I decided to organize the ride myself and involve other group homes in the project. At a monthly meeting of the state association for group homes, I introduced the idea to several other directors. It would involve the three of us once again riding from the ocean but ending at San Mar. Each day, we would stop at a different group home. When we did, the staff of that particular facility would plan an event around our arrival and invite the media. Most would then creatively use the event as a fundraiser for their facility.

As we were talking, Louise Richards, the director at the Maryland Salem Children's Trust in Grantsville overheard the conversation. She was intrigued and very much wanted to be included in the event. I knew that Grantsville was about fifteen miles past Frostburg in Garrett County. It was over a hundred miles west of San Mar with at least five mountains in between. Between Cumberland and Frostburg was a twelve mile long hill that would have to be conquered at the end of a long hard day of riding.

I saw the enthusiasm of Louise and suggested we plan on starting at Salem and ending at the ocean. She was delighted. The long uphill just became a long descent toward the start of the first day. Plans were made. Two other experienced riders joined us making it five who would go from Salem to the ocean over a five-day period. Along the way, we would stop at five different children's homes. It was named *The Five for Kids Project*. It would continue for several years. Over time, several other riders joined the group, and the name was changed to *Outspokin for Maryland's Kids*.

When the five of us arrived at San Mar during that first ride, the media was there waiting. A bull roast had been planned to welcome us and to encourage supporters to attend. There were about two hundred people cheering as we rolled in. Standing in the group was Ellen Savoy. At the time, Ellen was still a case worker with our Treatment Foster Care Program. Soon after watching the five ride in, Ellen approached me and announced she was going to do the ride the following year. At forty-five years of age and no history of doing any type of athletic activities, I was somewhat skeptical of her commitment. The ride over five mountains and a hundred plus miles was challenging even for experienced riders. "You are planning to ride from Salem to here next year?" I asked.

"No. *I will* ride from Salem to the ocean next year." She responded without hesitation. The following year, Ellen began preparing for the ride with fear and excitement driving and pulling her. As staff and residents saw Ellen commit to training on the bike, the story spread that she was going to do the ride with the men in September. No one held back in describing how difficult and challenging it was. A few questioned her sanity.

Ellen, however, went on to complete that ride all the way to the ocean. Her accomplishment was inspiring to many. Even to her, as it was only a short time after that she made the decision to enroll in graduate school and pursue a master's degree while continuing to work full time. I realized she had heard the same whisper Allie and I had heard at the top of a mountain, "What else can you do that you never dreamed possible?"

> I realized Ellen had heard the same whisper Allie and I had heard at the top of a mountain, "... What else can you do that you never dreamed possible?"

The following year, Ellen announced that she was going to do the ride a second time. This time we all believed her. It was at that point that Joni came to me and announced, "I'm gonna do it." It wasn't a question. She wasn't asking...actually she was, but as a conduct-disordered, oppositional angry fifteen-year old, she didn't want to appear as if she was asking for anything.

At fifteen, Joni already had a history of doing what she wanted, when she wanted. To the casual observer, it appeared as if her attitude had resulted in her placement and subsequent removal from numerous group facilities. In reality, it was the multiple traumas she had known in early childhood that had helped shape her combative demeanor, but few had recognized the connection.

Most recently, her frustrated father and stepmother had sent her to a wilderness program in Arizona for several months. It hadn't any more effect on her than the others.

Several months earlier, she had come to live in our Findlay Home. I had noticed how she had worked to expertly alienate almost all of the staff around her while setting herself up as the leader among the many girls in the program.

As I would listen to her and watch her interact with others, I realized she was a very intelligent girl. I had not read any of her records, but I suspected she had a very high IQ. She was failing in school but only because she had refused to study or even attend. She simply did not want to and could see no reason to go...and no one would make her.

"You're going to do what?" I asked her.

"I'm doing that bike ride."

It was a very demanding event with the first day covering over a hundred miles and five mountains. It was not a ride for a teenage girl who had no disciplined-exercise routine or physical conditioning at all and had never ridden a bicycle more than a couple of miles, if that. I had hoped she didn't know about Ellen.

"What ride?" She certainly wasn't talking about the ride to the ocean. "The one yer gonna do." It was stated as if she was reporting an obvious fact I was somehow failing to grasp. If her riding was a fact, it was one I really could not grasp. I refused to even consider such a proposal. Joni, however, had a streak of stubbornness within her that was deeper than I had envisioned. She refused to let go and questioned me about it relentlessly. I was beginning to understand why Chinese water torture was so effective. Eventually, I heard myself say to her, "Okay, Joni, if you attend school and have perfect attendance between now and the time of the ride (several months away), if you have straight As in all your classes (an easy attainment for her), if you have *no* behavior problems at school or here (maybe not such an easy attainment), and if you commit to begin an aggressive training program and stick to it, then I will take you out of school and allow you to join the ride for the entire week." I knew I was safe, and it would stop her petitioning me nonstop.

"I'll do it."…end of discussion. Joni attended school the next day. I never saw her studying or doing homework, but she produced the As. The behavior problems ceased. An aggressive training regimen commenced. She trained with Ellen.

When the truck, the hostage was driving, stopped and the passenger door opened, a bloodied Joni stepped out.

Shortly after, she began her training routine with Ellen; they found themselves at the top of South Mountain. It had been a long challenging climb to the top. After resting for a while, Ellen cautioned Joni that they needed to use care as they descended.

The road was fairly steep and somewhat winding. Never having been down the road before, Ellen advised Joni to go slowly and carefully. When they were ready to leave, Ellen pulled out first. Almost immediately, the road turned sharply to the left then immediately to the right. It was the steepest part of the hill.

Several minutes later when Ellen arrived at the bottom, she turned to see how Joni had enjoyed the exhilarating descent. When she did, she realized that she was alone. Joni was nowhere in sight.

For several minutes, she stood waiting as she wrestled with how to respond. Calling her on a cell phone wasn't an option. She realized as it would be several years before they were to be invented. Instead, she waited and prayed, hoping she was not going to have to climb back up the hill she had just descended.

Eventually, she saw an old pick-up truck coming down the hill. She decided to flag it down and ask if they had seen a young girl with a bicycle at the top or along the route.

As the truck drew near, she began waving at the driver to stop. However, he stopped the truck as soon as he saw her in the distance. When he did, the passenger door opened and a bloodied Joni stepped out, reached into the back of the truck and pulled out her bike. Ellen quickly approached the driver to learn what had happened. As she drew near, it was apparent; the driver had no desire to chat.

Joni had waited until Ellen had gone around the first turn before beginning her descent. As she neared the second turn, she was startled when a squirrel ran across the road. For an instant, she lost focus, and instead of making the turn, she drove off the road. She wasn't seriously hurt or even dissuaded. The scrapes on her leg would heal. The damage to the bike was minimal, but she wasn't sure about riding it down the hill in the condition it was in.

As she climbed back up to the road, she saw a pick-up truck coming down the hill toward her. When she did, she stood in the middle of the lane and pointed directly at the driver, magically willing the truck to come to a full stop. It did.

Then with no discussion, she opened the passenger door and told the startled driver that he was going take her to the bottom of the hill. With the door standing open, she lifted her bike into the back of the truck before sitting in the passenger seat and shutting the door. When they approached the bottom of the hill and the driver saw Ellen, he instantly recognized her as his rescuer and stopped at once. As Ellen approached the vehicle, she realized Joni was bleeding, and there was some damage to the bike. The driver remained behind the wheel, so she walked around to thank him for helping and to request he take them back to San Mar. However, as soon as the bike was out of the back of the truck, he sped off, the passenger door slamming along the way. The hostage was free.

I realized they had hired the petite young woman thinking she would not last. Little did they know they had hired the most determined person they would ever meet.

Ellen understood. She had seen the same look in the eyes of several staff when they had the opportunity to work with Joni. That incident didn't slow Joni down at all. She continued her training and even returned and climbed that hill again, without falling or taking any hostages. I took her out of school for a week; that was undoubtedly the turning point in her young life. She did the entire ride, and although it wasn't easy, she did keep up. She was very much a team player and never complained. I was absolutely proud of her. Joni remained with the program for over a year. It was the last group home she would ever live in. She returned to her father and step-mother's home...and dropped out of school.

Ten years later, I was having a conversation with one of our foster families. At the end of our meeting, the foster mother made a point of saying to me, "Joni says hi."

I wasn't sure who she meant. After so many years and hundreds of youth, I sometimes needed reminding. "Joni?"

"Joni…Surely you remember! I'm her stepmom. He's her dad." Oh my! Surely, I remember! No wonder they were such fine foster parents. They had been trained by fire. She went on to explain that Joni had dropped out of school, but the outrageous rebellion they had lived with earlier had ceased altogether. She had landed a position at PepsiCo in Frederick…unloading trucks. We laughed. I realized PepsiCo had hired the petite young woman thinking she would not last. Little did they know, they had hired the most determined person they would ever meet. Joni had outworked everyone there. When she realized they would pay her way through college, she went to night school to finish high school while working the job full time during the day. Once she had her GED in hand, she held them to their promise to pay for her college. She attended classes at night and eventually earned her degree. When Joni came by a few weeks later to see me, it was as a college graduate. Once again, I was truly proud of her accomplishments and not surprised.

In 2011, I organized a breakfast at the Hager Hall in Hagerstown. We had invited over two hundred persons to come to a free breakfast where I shared with them the dream of San Mar and asked them to help with generous contributions. Almost $50,000 was raised in the event. Part of it was due to the impact on the audience when Joni stood on the stage and shared her story. Prior to me speaking to the audience, she told the story of moving from group home to group home. She talked about the rage that had boiled out of her. Then she spoke about the life-changing connections made at San Mar. But it was after I spoke and shared the need for generous support, and she returned to the stage that she really surprised them. She went on to say how those connections had led to an entire change in her attitude and outlook on life. I realized that the entire room was viewing her as if she was still that teenage girl.

But I also realized Joni was standing before them, and it was her story she was telling. At twenty-eight years old, she had become the youngest General Manager for PepsiCo. She was also San Mar's newest board member and a college graduate. She would be starting her master's degree in a few months. Of course, PepsiCo would be paying for it. Once again, she held her audience captive.

This time it wasn't an angry Joni they saw but a determined Joni. People change. Over time, Joni completed her master's degree and continued to move up in the ranks of PepsiCo. She even served a term as the president of San Mar's board. Joni is now a married mother of three great kids. She is no longer the General Manager of the plant she had worked in unloading trucks. Instead, she became a successful executive overseeing some of PepsiCo's work in several Northeastern states. I recently asked Joni if she had met Indra Nooyi, the chair and CEO of PepsiCo and consistently ranked as one of the one hundred most powerful women in the world. Joni replied that they had not met yet, but that it was scheduled to happen in another month. I commented to her that I suspected she had it on her to do list to become the president and CEO of PepsiCo Worldwide. She didn't say anything, but she smiled. It was a smile I had seen before.

BEVERLY AND THE PURSUIT OF HAPPINESS

"I just want to be happy." I must admit that when Beverly made that statement, it took me awhile to realize the belief system underlying her declaration. I had heard kids say similar things many times over the years. Beverly was speaking on behalf of many. She just didn't know it. What a person believes is very important. It shapes who they are and drives what they do. Actually, I have come to understand that a person's beliefs are not always revealed by what they say. A person's true beliefs are revealed by their actions. To understand what a person believes, I need to listen intently to what they say and watch closely what they do.

Over the years, as I would sit and listen to countless youth, I began to observe there was a common belief system among them. I also realized that if I were to sit down with a teen and ask her to explain to me what she believed about life, she would have to really think about it for a while. The reason is that most have typically not thought through what they believe.

However, after having thought about it, she would tell me a few of the things, which she believed to be important. I suspect most of the items I observed as part of a common belief system would not be on the list with what she would share with me. I realize that is not because such beliefs are not true; rather because they are so familiar to her, she doesn't recognize them. She is so close to them she doesn't see them. The other observation I made was related to those persons I hired to work directly with the youth. Keep in mind that most of the youth who came to us had known trauma in their lives. They had known hurts and often responded by hurting others. Usually, such hurting was verbal and emotional and often caught the new staff off guard.

As I would listen to the inexperienced staff, I realized that just as the youth themselves often failed to realize there was a common belief system among them so did the staff. That is, staff would tend to address youth from their own reference points, not realizing the youth typically had very little genuine interest in their perspective whatsoever. As I thought about it, expecting a teen to understand my perspective might be somewhat challenging. It might be more effective if I sought to help them recognize and understand their own beliefs. It might be even more effective if I helped the new staff understand the youth they were working with and how to communicate.

Below is a list of what I have found to be some of the key beliefs that tend to be fairly common in the youth who have come to us. The challenge is how to effectively communicate with those who hold such beliefs.

The Top Ten

1. Disrespect me and I will give it back. I usually won't initiate it either way because then I have to think about what I believe. However, if you disrespect me, you give me a free ticket to disrespect you. Value me and you confuse me, and I don't know how to process it. You might as well speak to me in Russian. I just want to be happy.

2. Happiness is the result of being able to make my own decisions and occurs when I get to that place where adults stop telling me what to do. It is synonymous with being free to do what I want, when I want, and with whom I want. It's only reasonable!

3. My value is created by what others believe about me. What my peers think about me is more important than what adults think but is often hindered by what I think about myself.

4. Everything is someone else's fault. I am not to blame and not responsible. Don't even suggest otherwise. I won't listen.

5. Everything should be fair unless it is to my advantage not to be, then it doesn't matter…deal with it.

6. The truth is negotiable. There are no absolutes. Say whatever you can get away with at the time. Lying to adults really doesn't count. They don't understand my reality.

7. If I want it, then I should be able to have it. Live for today. Tomorrow will take care of itself. What is important is the here and now, leading to a constant pursuit of instant gratification. It is about happiness! It is about me.

8. The highest of human values and experiences is personal satisfaction and pleasure. I am entitled to my share of pleasure and comfort in my pursuit of happiness.

9. I must constantly be vigilant that my "needs" will be met, or someone else will take what should be mine.

10. Bigger pleasure is always better—a constant desire for greater, more effective stimulation is normal.

It is important to realize that these beliefs are not built upon reason or future planning, but on an existentialism found only in the present. They are not built on hope, which is always future focused. In 2012, I went to Peru with my son and several others and hiked the Inca Trail to Machu Pichu. During the hike, I learned from one woman who accompanied our group that she had a tremendous amount of personal debt that was creating a great deal of stress in her life. When I spoke with her, she admitted how difficult it had been for her to function with so much stress. She explained she was doing the hike as a means of addressing the stress. To her, it was the responsible thing to do. To me, it appeared she was ignoring a source of her stress and increasing her problem. I strongly suspected her stress would be waiting for her when she got back to reality. It was.

I told her that I understood how important it was to deal with stress; however, I questioned if hiking the Inca Trail was really a good solution as it was quite an expensive adventure, which she had paid for with her credit card.

She explained that she deserved a vacation like this, and she was not going to deprive herself simply because she was short on funds.

She was thirty-two at the time. I realized that the beliefs I was seeing in adolescents in the child welfare and juvenile justice systems may be much more widespread than I originally imagined.

The average American holds 52 percent more debt today than they did a decade ago. In 2017, the average household debt in America was $10,955 or $2,300 per person.[6] To be certain, credit is not the problem, as many handle it very responsibly. Rather, it is the beliefs one holds that allows credit to become an anvil holding them down. Actions reveal beliefs.

Teens, like everyone else, want to live life stress free. That seems pretty understandable, even reasonable. However, such stress-free liv-

___
[6] According to research conducted by the firm ValuePenguin for insurance companies across the United States.

ing occurs, so her unspoken reasoning goes when she finally arrives at the place where all the adults in her life stop telling her what to do; when she can get outside of the fence, others have erected around her. It is a place called happiness, or so it is believed. It is the goal of many, few ever arrive. Even America's child welfare system itself unwittingly reinforces this belief with the focus on preparing kids for independent living.

What if *happiness* really was a place, an actual destination! Over the years, I have spoken with, and listened to, many girls who have desperately wanted to find happiness only to learn they were looking in the wrong direction.

Consider the lessons from the small Himalayan kingdom of Bhutan, near Tibet and China, where marketing campaigns read "Happiness is a Place" and "Where Happiness Matters the Most."

In 1972, the king of Bhutan made a statement in an interview with a reporter that "the Gross National Happiness of their people was far more important than the Gross National Product of their nation." Thirty-six years later in 2008, the new king instituted a philosophy and practices that guides the government in measuring the collective happiness and well-being of the population.

Bhutan is a small nation of only 900,000 people. There are no stoplights in the nation. There is one escalator. It is located in a mall in the capital. All tobacco and tobacco products are banned as are all plastic bags. Polygamy and polyandry (a woman with multiple husbands) are both legal. Only eight pilots in the entire world are authorized to fly into the one international airport. There is only one double-lane road in the country. Bhutan was the last nation in the world to have television and one of the last to have internet.

The Gross National Happiness of the citizens was initially measured in 2008 as the first year of the ambitious project was underway. That in-depth survey was followed by a second one in 2010 and a third nationwide survey in 2015. The survey covered the entire nation and results were reported for varying demographic factors such as gender, age, and occupation. The first surveys consisted of long questionnaires that polled the citizens about living conditions and religious behavior, including questions about the number of times a person prayed in a day. Bhutan is primarily a Buddhist nation.

As a result of measuring happiness, an action plan was created that has been credited as being one of the major variables in a reduction in poverty from 23 percent in the sixties to 8.2 percent in 2017, with a goal of 5 percent projected for the end of 2018.

Crime although very low by Western standards, has been on the rise and has been attributed to being a result of the influence of television and the new found desire for the materialism of the west.

However, even in this land of happiness, there have been critics looking closely at how several of the goals were attained. According to Human Rights Watch, "Over 100,000 of the population of Nepalese origin and Hindu faith were expelled from the country because they would not integrate with Bhutan's Buddhist culture."[7]

The Refugee Council of Australia stated that, "It is extraordinary and shocking that a nation can get away with expelling one sixth of its people and somehow keep its international reputation as a land of happiness."[8]

In an article written in the Economist magazine, "The Himalayan kingdom of Bhutan is not in fact an idyll in a fairy tale. It is home to perhaps 900,000 people most of whom live in grinding poverty."[9] Other criticism cites "increasing levels of political corruption,

---

[7] Human Rights Watch
https://www.hrw.org/news/2008/02/01/bhutans-ethnic-cleansing

[8] The Australian Refugee Council https://www.refugeecouncil.org.au/media/time-to-challenge-bhutans-gross-national-hypocrisy/

[9] The Economist Magazine
http://www.economist.com/node/3445119

the rapid spread of diseases such as aids and tuberculosis, gang violence, abuses against women and ethnic minorities, shortages in food/medicine, and economic woes."[10]

I have listened to many who have wanted to be at the destination of happiness. Instead, they learned as they went along, what they thought was the path to that end was, in reality, a dead end.

Bhutan responds to such criticisms by pointing out that happiness is a process of development and learning, rather than an absolute end point. They are aspiring to enhance the happiness of its people and Gross National Happiness efforts serve as a measurement tool for realizing that aspiration. Maybe so, but the national marketing material call it "the Land of Happiness" and invite people to come. That is, if they have their visits preauthorized and only enter the country with an approved travel company and fly in with one of the eight approved pilots.

I was reminded once again of my journey to Independence Pass in the Colorado Rockies. When I started, I thought it was about getting to the destination. When I arrived at the top of the mountain, I realized it was really about the journey.

10 The GSD Magazine
https://www.gsdmagazine.org/the-false-promises-of-bhutans-gross-national-happiness/

Maybe happiness is not the physical location that so many have been seeking. If that is the case, then what is the destination we should be moving toward?

To the many youth who believed *happiness* to be the place outside the boundaries of adult authority where they had the freedom to make their own decisions and do what they want, it has often ended up as a place of emptiness. I have listened to many who have wanted to be at the destination of happiness. Instead, they learned as they went along, what they thought was the path to that end was, in reality, a dead end.

To the caring adult in a youth's life the focus needs to be on empowering the teen to successfully cross the bridge from adolescence (or living within the boundaries of safety and common sense) to adulthood. It is a focus on teaching the life skills necessary to be successful within a safe and supportive context. It is a good and responsible course of action.

The teen, however, often hears the call to independence differently. It is a paradigm far different from that held by the adults working to transfer the skills. To the girl waiting for the moment she can step outside the boundaries set by the various adults in her life, the call to independence is too often heard as a call to self-centeredness. In her paradigm, others exist to facilitate meeting her needs on her journey to stepping outside the fence completely. What she fails to understand is that 100 percent of healthy living comes from living inside the appropriate boundaries.

A recent visit with my son offered a great example as to why living within such boundaries can be genuinely freeing. It is a lesson that makes no sense until experienced.

LIFE ON THE LINE

The Story of Roo and Shey

Since early childhood, my youngest son, Dan, has had a God-Given talent for working with dogs. Over the years, that gift has combined with a sincere love and extensive experience to produce an insight and understanding that has made him a sought after dog coach and handler. For many years, Dan has lived in Truckee, California, near Lake Tahoe, where he has shared his knowledge and abilities with the dogs of the Truckee Police Department and the Humane Society. It was there that he first met Roo, a beautiful black Labrador retriever.

Roo was approximately six months old the first time they met. When first brought into the shelter, Roo would spend much of her time cowered in a corner. It was evident to those who saw her that she had known abuse. Dan later described her, upon entering the shelter, as being the most damaged dog he had encountered from among the thousands he had worked with over the years. However, as he sought to gain her trust, he was able to see what she could become and fell in love with her. Four days later, he adopted her.

He realized that for her to experience healing, he would need to build a solid foundation of trust so she could move past her fears. He also understood trust begins with full acceptance, from which everyday routines and practices flow. As Dan began the journey of establishing a life-long relationship with Roo, he would take her to a remote location near Truckee where the distractions were limited. It was there he introduced her to the boundaries imposed by a twenty-foot leash. Dan explained that dogs need security (the knowledge and feeling that they are safe). Once they learn to trust and feel secure, they will then accept leadership that is consistent. Trust flows when the dog believes it is valued and secure. As I listened to Dan, I couldn't help note the comparisons to the many youths I had known. As they walked in those early days, Roo would see something ahead and run to the limits of the leash until she was tugging for Dan to release it or run himself. It was at that point, Dan would change his direction forcing Roo to refocus on him and what he was doing. Within a few twenty-minute sessions, Roo was staying within a few feet of Dan as they walked without him holding the leash tight. It was important for Dan to have Roo's full attention if she was going to change her behavior. As the days and weeks went by and Roo's trust of Dan increased, Roo's attention was evidenced by her staying closer to him and following his every move as they walked. At that point, he switched to a short leash and eventually to no leash at all as she consistently walked by his side.

Recently, I had the opportunity to spend some time with Roo and Dan at their home in Truckee. Several mornings, we would walk to a nearby lake and then follow the path all the way around the lake. Each time my oldest son, Kit, would accompany us with another dog, Shey. Roo trusts Dan implicitly and follows his every command without a leash; although much older, Shey is just learning to trust and still requires his leash.

Several times during my time with my sons, we would jump in the car and go somewhere for the day. Roo was usually accompanying us. Depending on where we were going, Shey would often remain at the house since he had not yet progressed to the point that he was able to control his own behavior, nor had he come to the point of realizing the need to do so. Dan explained that through his consistency as a trainer, the dog would bring his own behavior in line. Shey would experience personal growth and freedom to the degree Dan was consistent in providing appropriate boundaries.

Toward the end of my visit, Dan invited Kit and me to join him at the opening night of the nearby Reno Aces baseball team. As a season ticket holder, Dan was able to get some pretty good seats. It was an exciting game. The home team (Dan's team) was winning ten to one. Somewhere into the seventh inning, I noticed that a couple of rows in front of us was a family of four. Mom was pretty focused on the box of popcorn in her lap while dad appeared to be following the game. The two children, probably ages three and four, had long since lost any focus on the game and were having a wonderful time playing on the concrete stairs at the end of the row.

> Shey would experience personal growth and freedom to the degree Dan was consistent in providing appropriate boundaries.

They weren't bothering anyone, that is, until a line of people under the leadership of a woman with an extra-large box of popcorn started down the stairs and was forced to stop or risk stepping on the children. Although the kids realized the pending problem, they remained in the center of the aisle watching the woman holding the extra-large box of popcorn. They were, no doubt, watching as I was, to see if she was going to spill popcorn all over the steps. Within moments, dad realized that his parenting skills were needed. Without moving, he looked at the kids and in a very serious "I'm not kidding" voice ordered both kids back to their seats.

Whereas, I could hear him clearly from three rows away, the kids apparently did not from only four feet away. The popcorn lady and the line behind her remained in place, as did the kids. As I watched mom, who was sitting one seat away from where the kids were, continue her focus on her own popcorn. Dad glanced back over a second time, and once again ordered them to clear the aisle and get back in their seats. This time the kids heard him…probably. They both instantly moved to the far side of the stairs to let the line of grown-ups pass. However, as soon as the line went by, as if on cue from an unseen choreographer, the older child began heading up the stairs while the younger began descending. I noticed that dad had already returned to the game since the problem had been resolved, and his skills were no longer on display. Mom's focus remained consistently focused on the popcorn. I envisioned Shey pulling at the long leash wanting to investigate all the interesting sights and smells yet often being left behind because of his lack of control. Dan had mentioned that the most challenging aspect of working with dogs was teaching the humans how to be consistent, trustworthy, and focused.

I realized the father in front of me thought the problem was with his kids playing in the aisle and what others, subsequently, thought about him as a parent. I wasn't quite sure what mom was thinking. In reality, the problem appeared to be that they did not seem to be building trust with their kids in a manner that revealed to the kids the inherent value they have. I also realized the parents had no clue as to the seriousness of what was happening. In a few years, when the kids had grown into teenagers, I envisioned mom and dad wondering what happened all of a sudden.

Dan was producing very credible results with the many dogs he was training. It was through the consistency he was showing, yet the mom at the game had also shown consistency in her focus on her popcorn as her kids played, and her husband took charge. I realized that for consistency to be effective and to form a foundation for authentic trust, it has to be free of contradictions. As I watched, I suspected dad was being consistent as to how he often dealt with the children's behaviors, yet when there was no follow-through, or a message affirming the value in each child, his message was being viewed as contradictory and; subsequently, not to be taken seriously. As the children continue to age and the same parenting practices are followed, the parents are likely to become more controlling as they believe others are evaluating them as a result of their kids' behaviors, or they will become more distant and uninvolved, especially if they don't see the kids responding to their control.

For consistency to be effective and to form a foundation for authentic trust it has to be free of contradictions. Good intentions don't create forward motion and changed lives.

I realized that if I want to be taken seriously I have to be consistent without contradictions, and when I am not, I must be honest about it and take ownership. Consistency builds patterns and creates momentum. Therefore, when there are contradictions present, it is wise to address them in such a manner that you can be taken seriously moving forward. Consistent behaviors are a reflection of what you value and can breed respect and credibility over the long run, or the opposite becomes truth. Good intentions don't produce the desired outcomes over time.

As I flew home, the flight attendant stood toward the front of the plane and went through the preflight instructions that most of her captive audience had heard many times. When she came to the part about the oxygen mask dropping down, she said, "When in the course of our flight there is a drop in cabin pressure, an oxygen mask will drop down from the space above your head. If you are traveling with a child, or someone needing your assistance, put the mask on yourself first."

I envisioned someone trying to put an oxygen mask on a child and passing out because they hadn't taken the time to put their own on first. They wanted to do the right thing but went about it all wrong. I thought about Anya running away to go help her siblings but totally running in the wrong direction. Good intentions don't create forward motion and changed lives. Dan had shared how many people would come to him with out of control dogs. They wanted him to fix the undisciplined animal for them. He would gently explain that until they could master their own behaviors and provide consistent and appropriate boundaries, the dog was not going to feel secure, and the trust needed would never be complete. They needed to put the mask on themselves first. I had repeatedly seen the same thing in working with the girls in my group homes.

For years, I would have sincere and well-meaning people come to me looking for work. Many wanted desperately to make a difference in the life of a hurting child. Over time, I came to understand that if I was going to have a strong and effective team who could genuinely impact the lives of kids who had known trauma, I would do better questioning the candidates as to how they were taking care of themselves and assuming responsibility for their own lives. This would be more valuable than trying to learn what they knew (or thought they knew) about working with kids.

Some skills I could teach them; however, if they had not learned self-discipline by the time they came to me, they were in the wrong place. As the flight attendant had so correctly stated, they needed to put the oxygen mask on themselves first if they ever wanted to help someone else. I heard Beverly's words in my mind, "I just want to be happy. Why does everything seem to go wrong?" Because, Beverly, you are thinking that happiness is a destination. In reality, it is found in the journey itself as you learn to live within appropriate boundaries. Beverly and the "instant on" generation can't understand why happiness just doesn't happen when they step outside the boundaries imposed by the adults around them. The belief is that happiness is waiting for them. It is therefore, important that the adults in a youth's life take ownership for their lives and then take the required time to connect, teach, and model that 100 percent of healthy living takes place within appropriate boundaries. The results can be life changing.

ZOEY AND THE
DEATH SPIRAL

Zoey was distraught. I could see it as soon as I sat down with her. Our staff exceeded 120 persons. As a result, I didn't usually get involved in direct problem solving with the girls. However, Zoey was distraught and requested to speak with me personally. I knew that one of the most important things anyone can do for an adolescent is to listen, so I sat down and gave Zoey my undivided attention. She proceeded to pour out her story about how she had lost the opportunity to go on an outing that she had been looking forward to for so long. Now, due to the actions of my staff, she explained, her hopes had been dashed. She was heartbroken and was hoping that I would make everything right by overruling all of the misguided decisions that had led to this point.

After Zoey finished her heart wrenching story, I asked her a few questions to help me understand a little better. It seemed she had forgotten to mention a few of the details when sharing her story with me. I have noticed that can happen quite easily. It is important to ask the right questions. As we discussed the situation, I shared my observation with her. Whereas, it had appeared to her the staff overreacted to what she had done; it appeared to me that underlying issues of lying and stealing apparently had been driving this particular incident. I didn't need to remind her that it was those particular issues that had worked together to bring her to us in the first place. If they had been serious enough to have her removed from her family, it seemed to follow that we should be paying attention now. In fact, she had worked with the treatment team to develop a personal plan of action to help her take responsibility for her issues and her life. That plan, which she helped to develop, involved zero tolerance for lying and stealing. Put in that context she stated, "I am so upset. I promised myself that I wouldn't lie or steal again as long as I was here."

As I listened to her words, I realized that she was speaking from her heart. I also recognized she was a *renter* and not an *owner*. She had placed her entire focus on doing whatever she had to do to get out and get home. At the same time, she was not at all concerned about understanding and changing those things that had resulted in her problems in the first place. Those issues had been defined as problem areas by others, not her. In reality, she probably never took the time to think about it because to do so would force her to look back to some rather painful experiences in her life. With the past in turmoil, looking toward the future with any clarity was often difficult.

One trait common to youth in crisis is the lack of vision. They can't see into the future because they are trying to cope with the present. To those motorists passing me as I pedaled to the top of Independence Pass, I appeared motionless. It is also true that when a youth is unable to see into the future, they lack hope. When Zoey was placed into our care, the agency placing her began paying a daily rate to help with her care. She was in fact renting space (with others paying the rent) until she had conformed enough to everyone's expectations that they would leave her alone and let her go home (where there was very little structure, and she could do as she pleased…again).

Too often success is measured by what appears to look good. Our ability to show that the girls in our care are well-behaved tends to make the organization look good. However, making the organization look good somehow was left out of our outcome measures or mission statement. Instead, the focus was set on helping kids today to become productive members of society tomorrow. For that to occur, they must be able to recognize and accept responsibility for their own actions. My conversation with several ladies visiting the campus pointed that out. One of them commented to me that she knew San Mar was a very fine and successful organization. I suspect every director likes to hear such glowing praise, so I thanked her and asked her, what it was exactly that gave her such an impression of the fine job we were doing. Without missing a beat, she stated that she had heard it from many others and had now been here to see for herself. She saw how clean the facility was; she noted how well-groomed the lawns were; all of the girls she had met were well-behaved and so polite. I thanked her and told her we certainly try to do a good job. Then I smiled and asked her if she knew that 70 percent of the girls leaving our programs were arrested within six months, and that 50 percent of them were pregnant within a year.

The look of instant and genuine shock on the entire group of ladies shouted, "Awkward…"

The stunned looks appearing on the faces of each lady in the small group conveyed discomfort and confusion. Slowly, I explained that what I said was not true. However, my point was that too often, we measure success by how things look. Doing so can lead to deep problems. Progress and success doesn't always appear pretty. The doorway to meaningful connections isn't always through smiles, beauty, and being polite. Those are without doubt nice, but ten years from now, will they have contributed to lasting change that is still evident?

> Without hope, there are no dreams. There is no ownership of their own lives. There is no reason to even try. A hopeless person sees himself as motionless.

Through Zoey's statement of disappointment with herself, she was telling me that she had found lying and stealing to work for her, and she would go back to them as soon as she was discharged. They were what she knew and was comfortable using. They worked for her, or so she reasoned. She had not connected the dots to realize that those particular behaviors were in reality destroying her. She realized she had made a mistake. She got caught. The next time, she simply wouldn't allow herself to get caught. Were we helping her to become a productive member of society later on in life, or were we simply using her to help maintain jobs for all of us as she served time?

It was imperative that we develop owners; youth who began the process of taking charge of their own lives so that upon discharge, they could continue the process of moving into adulthood.

We had to give vision!

Zoey's statement of regret for failing to meet her own expectations reflects a complete lack of personal ownership for her actions. She promised herself that she would conform to the norms of the system so the adults in her life would leave her alone. To many of the adults in her life, conformity to their structure appeared as a successful outcome... but was it really? She was compliant, but her heart and mind were not changed.

Making a person conform to a structure they have no ownership in whatsoever is possible. It is a control model and quite useful when trying to produce immediate safety and stability. It is less effective when trying to produce lasting results.

When a youth enters any of our programs with what has been defined as out of control behaviors, which have proven to be destructive to her, it is important to first help her gain control of her life. For that to occur, it is necessary to provide an age appropriate structure that addresses her specific needs. The focus must, at some point, move from helping gain control of the destructive behaviors, to helping find ownership and forward motion.

If the focus remained on controlling her behaviors, a disservice would be done. Zoey had initially believed we were making a really big deal over something that was in reality only annoying, but not the major issue we had seemed to suggest.

Once again my son, Dan, provided a great object lesson that enabled Zoey and me a much greater understanding as to the importance of a person taking ownership for their life. Before Dan ever began school, my wife expressed a strong desire to home school both of our boys. At the time, home schooling was just beginning to take root, and there was still a great deal of uncertainty among many as to its effectiveness. However, she believed that by giving the boys personal attention, we could bring out and build upon the apparent strengths in each. As we began the adventure, we continued seeking to identify their budding interests so as to develop and build upon them. On the fourth Saturday of each month, San Mar's Volunteer Association would hold a meeting and typically have some type of program for the girls in our group homes. On one particular Saturday, they had invited the manager from a flight school at the local airport that offered flying lessons. When she came, she not only spoke with enthusiasm and held her youthful audience in rapt attention, she also brought along a mobile flight simulator used in training new pilots. After she spoke, each of the girls were given the opportunity to fly the simulator.

> The focus must, at some point, move from helping gain control of the destructive behaviors, to helping find ownership and forward motion.

For many years, we had lived in a home on the San Mar campus that the board had provided for us. As a result, the boys would often attend such presentations, which they thought might be interesting. Typically, they would sit in the back of the room and not participate in the discussions. On this occasion, however, Dan was drawn in by her presentation and had already begun envisioning himself flying. When the simulator was brought out and offered to the group, the boys remained in the background until it was clear the girls were finished and ready to leave.

It was then the speaker saw them standing in the back and challenged them to try out the simulator. Such an offer only needed to be extended once.

To Kit, the simulator was interesting and fun, but to Dan, it was magnetic. It did not go unnoticed that he was also very good at it. She gave him some literature and encouraged him to come out to the airport where she would arrange for him to have a free flight lesson.

Within a few days, we made the arrangements and visited the airport. As she promised, Dan was given the free lesson, and the hook was in.

It wasn't very long before we were figuring out the particulars as to how to make the payments for all the lessons that flowed from the free one. We also needed to figure out how to get him back and forth. He was still too young to drive a car. As the lessons progressed, Dan excelled. He loved to fly. He particularly enjoyed flying solo and would often circle above the house and campus to make his presence known. However, in order to successfully complete the course, he needed to pass the stalls.

The instructor had explained to him exactly what was going to take place. They were going to take the plane up with Dan flying. At ten thousand feet, Dan would take the plane into a very steep climb. Eventually as they climbed, the engine would stop.

When it did, the plane would immediately begin to fall toward the earth. The instructor continued that; for Dan to recover, he would need to reduce the angle of attack to that which would again produce lift by moving the control column forward to pitch the nose down. That action would cause a loss of height so he could apply full power to minimize the loss. Of course, he would need to control the consequent yaw by applying rudder.

It was absolutely imperative that Dan understand exactly the instructions that were being given to him because there would only be a window of about eight seconds in which he needed to restart the engine, or they would find themselves drawn into a "death spiral." If the instructions were not absolutely clear, he had to make it known.

The instructor explained it was called a death spiral because pulling out of it was highly unlikely. Therefore, as soon as the engine shut off, it would become Dan's responsibility, as the student, to restart it and to fly out of the fall. If after five seconds, the instructor explained, Dan failed to respond and restart the engine, the instructor would take over. There would be no discussion. Dan would fail the test.

> Even though Zoey had never piloted a plane, she was at high risk for falling into a death spiral.
>
> Her refusal to acknowledge and accept personal responsibility for her actions had far reaching consequences that she was not seeing.

Mastering this skill was mandatory for any pilot. Some airline crashes in recent years have shown how important the early learning of stall recovery can prevent a future catastrophe.

The instructor later told Dan after successfully completing the challenge, that more students dropped out of flight school when they faced falling from the sky in a death spiral during stalls than at any other time.

As Dan related his experience to me, I envisioned myself explaining to Zoey her need to take ownership of her lying and stealing. Failure to master those weaknesses would result in a death spiral. It was vital that she understand what I was trying to communicate to her. I realized that in all likelihood, she would not tell me if what I said to her was not understood. Clarity in communication was important. Sometimes the instructor needed to step in and start the engine. It prevented a crash, but it did not create an independent and competent pilot. To be an independent pilot, the student, at some point, had to assume the responsibility of actually starting the engine themselves and flying out of the fall. It could be terrifying even when you know it's coming but so are the alternatives.

I was comforted to see that Dan grasped that truth.

TRINA: PUTTING ON THE WAR PAINT

Abram Maslow was a psychologist who gained more than fifteen minutes of fame in 1943 when he published an article entitled "Theory of Human Motivation" in the scientific journal, *Psychological Review*.

In the article, he defined a hierarchy of needs each person must master in their journey through life. Each stage is dependent upon the needs of the previous stage being met. For example, a starving person will have a difficult time finding fulfillment in their relationships until the need for food has been met. The woman facing creditors trying to repossess her car is going to have a difficult time being able to focus effectively on being a contributing member of a team, caring for adolescents with their own unique needs while she is threatened with the loss of her own car. At the foundation of his pyramid, Maslow identified physiological issues. At the top was self-actualization. The self-actualized person would have safety, health, and security issues met and would be free to deal with much more abstract issues of life such as meaning and fulfillment.

However, as Maslow aged, he added a sixth stage to his pyramid and suggested that there may be another stage beyond self-actualization. He defined this stage as that of self-transcendency. In this stage, the individual has come to the realization that the world does not revolve around them. They are able to set aside their own self-interests for the good of others. There is an awareness of a bigger picture. It was, Maslow realized, the healthiest and strongest of all the stages of development, but it wasn't until he experienced people in his life modeling it, that he even perceived it as a possibility. It did not appear to be logical. To the adolescent with the desire to step outside the fence, it absolutely makes no sense. Maybe not, but Steven Covey in 1989 seemed to reinforce the need to grow beyond one's self-absorption when he addressed the stages of human development a little differently.[11]

Covey saw each person as being born totally dependent on others. As the child grew, they progressed to stages of independence. For example, when the infant reached the point of being able to sit up independently, it was a good thing and an evidence of healthy growth. However, even then, there were still numerous areas in their life where they remained dependent on others. When she started walking, she still needed help with those diapers.

As the child continued to grow, they would reach differing plateaus where they would exert themselves and attain independence. As they learned to walk without holding onto momma's hand, it was good. As they mastered feeding themselves, it was good. Therefore, Covey observed, independence was a healthy stage of development that never fully arrived on any one day but was continuous and progressive over many years as the brain continued to develop.

In adolescence, the process continues with different issues being addressed. Having long since mastered the basics of walking, talking, and feeding themselves, the adolescent is now maturing to the point of learning to make more complex decisions. They are learning to be responsible in a different context. Now, they have moved from mommy and family being the primary influencers in their lives to their peers taking on a greater role as their world expands. Covey suggests that if the focus remains on attaining independence during this stage, a true disservice has been done. Instead, youth must be taught that, in reality, there is another stage. That stage must be reached if one is to ever truly experience healthy living and eventually find that elusive happiness. Covey calls it "Interdependence." To the self-absorbed

---

[11] Stephen Covey, Seven Habits of Highly Effective People, 1989, Free Press.

youth focused on living independently, such a concept is meaningless. However, Covey suggests that we are in fact social beings and that to live successfully in society with others is to acknowledge our social reality and understand the need for a healthy give and take.

Interdependence, then, is that place where an individual is able to transcend their own desires for the benefit of the community of which they are a part. It is about assuming personal responsibility for one's actions. As demonstrated by Maslow, these lessons are best learned when modeled to a youth by caring adults in their lives who have learned these lessons themselves. Zoey and Anya were both illustrations of youth who struggled with personal ownership and interdependence in their lives. There were also many youths who understood. Trina was one of the best examples.

Trina had seen the signs strategically placed throughout the school. For at least two weeks, she had known a special speaker was coming. Each day as she passed the sign near the cafeteria, she found herself imagining what traveling to another country must be like. She had thought just moving to San Mar in Boonsboro, a rural community with cows and tractors, had been difficult and pretty foreign. Yet as the days passed, she found herself continuously thinking about what it might be like to live in another country while attending high school. It was something she had never considered. She decided to go and hear what he had to say but with some very mixed feelings. As an eleventh grader living in a group home, she realized the chances of her being able to do something like this were pretty slim. When the day arrived, she went to the meeting. The speaker made it clear that living in another country while attending high school was something most people never had the opportunity to do. It wasn't just group home kids that didn't have that chance given to them. He let them know that if they were part of this program and visited another country, they would return with new knowledge, cultural understanding, maturity, and lifelong friends from the host country. The hardest part would be leaving the host family and returning. The family will have shared in the adventure and learned from the student as much as the student would have learned from them. She would only be gone for a school year, but the experience would enrich the rest of her life.

Life in her own family had been traumatic. She and her sister had known the horror of abuse. She had talked about it. Her sister had not. It appeared her sister had been victimized to a much greater extent. Trina wasn't so sure that was true. Trina knew what they had suffered and had made the decision to talk about it with others who she thought cared deeply and could help her. Her sister would not. It was too painful. As time went on, Trina found herself forming new friendships that would last. The grip the abuse had held on her mind was decreasing. The thought of being a part of a family, even temporarily, both pulled at her and repelled her at the same time. She sat near the front of the room, and as the man talked about the program, she found her mind flooded with questions. How do you know the families are safe? Will other kids be there? What if I can't speak the language? What if I want to come back early? What if I simply hate it?

> She saw his hesitation and felt it. Her excitement drained instantly. She had seen the reaction before and realized she was being stereotyped. She recognized the familiar feelings of anger welling up within. She spoke directly to the issue. "Is that a problem?"

He had given everyone the opportunity to ask questions throughout the meeting; However, she had waited until the meeting was over, and he had finished his presentation. It was then she went to him and began asking her questions.

He clearly saw her interest and tried to fully answer every question she asked. That is, until she revealed to him that she was living in a group home. She had been removed from her own family due to some difficulties. His hesitation upon learning she was a group home girl was imperceptible to most. Trina was not most. She saw his hesitation and felt it. Her excitement drained instantly. She had seen such a reaction many times before and recognized she was being stereotyped. She recognized the familiar feelings of anger welling up within. She spoke directly to the issue. "Is that a problem?"

"Well, it might be. We have never had a student from a group home ever participate in the program. We have had some inquiries, but as they look into it, they tend to find there are just too many obstacles. You are certainly welcome to take an application with you but keep in mind there have been quite a few others who have started the process only to find it is pretty difficult to work through."

When Trina returned from school that day, it was evident that something had happened. The typically vivacious teen appeared withdrawn. Something had happened, but no one seemed to know what. I approached her and asked if she had some time we could speak.

She did.

Initially, she wasn't sharing her heart. Everything was fine. However, as we sat there, I assured her that I was glad everything was going well but was confused as I was getting some mixed messages. Her words told me everything was fine, but her heart was telling me she was in pain.

I assured her that she didn't have to share anything, but if she decided she wanted to talk, then I was ready to listen. At that point, I was ready to end our conversation. She was not. At first, she shared slowly, then it became a flood.

She told me about the meeting at school. She related the details of the program and how it sounded so exciting. She talked about seeing the signs for two weeks and how she had begun thinking about going to another country as a student, a lot. She shared how he had answered all her questions. We laughed about how she thought Boonsboro had been the end of the world. She had never heard of anyone driving a tractor to school before coming. She couldn't say that anymore.

Then the laughing stopped as she hesitantly recalled the conversation when he learned she was a group home girl. Although he never said it or even suggested, she had felt stereotyped as bad and broken. Whereas she knew she was neither. It was really hard not to feel like it when he stood right there silently projecting something all over her that made her feel it inside and out. She admitted that part of what made her so angry was she knew he was right. Not that she was bad, he never said that, but that there were lots of obstacles. There were so many obstacles that no one had ever done it before, at least not in his program.

"Trina," I offered, "he might be absolutely right. The obstacles may be so many and so big that they can't be knocked down. I simply don't know. What I do know is that you have a choice at this point right here to accept that as truth and stop or to challenge it and proceed. You can try to climb the walls that hold you back."

> Although he never said it, or even suggested, she had felt stereotyped as bad and broken. Whereas she knew she was neither. It was really hard not to feel like it when he stood right there silently projecting something all over her that made her feel it inside and out.

"How can I challenge it? He has already told me that it can't happen!"

I continued, "Actually, what you said was he told you how all the others had given up and accepted the reality that the barriers could not be moved. He never told you that any of them tried to move the barriers. Even if he believes the barriers can't be moved, his belief doesn't make it truth. Does it? It seems to me that we can make a list of all the reasons this can't happen. It might be a long list. Then we can cry about how unfair life is as we look at the long list…or we can see if together we can begin knocking down those obstacles. If we can't, maybe we can climb over them. At least then we will know he was right if we fail."

She sat silently in front of me. I realized she was processing what I had said to her. Then without hesitation she began, "The Department of Social Services won't even allow me to leave the state without written permission. How will I ever get them to allow me to leave the country? I have to have parental permission and signatures on all their forms. I don't even know where my mother is, and if I did, I can't imagine her ever signing them? It will cost at least $2,500, and I don't have *any* money!"

As she continued, I interrupted her. I needed to know if I should be working up a good cry or writing them down for the list we were going to use as our declaration of war.

For a moment, she almost smiled and suggested we begin writing them down. We were going to need to develop action plans for each one. We were going to war! Maybe the first step was going to be some fresh war paint! This would not be a war fought in secret. It was a long list, but by the time we finished, I realized her entire demeanor had changed. She was not the victim she had been when she returned from school. She had become a resilient fighter, and she was breathing hope. Hope didn't guarantee success, but it created vision that led to ownership and action.

Over the next several months, we tackled each challenge one at a time. We convinced her social worker and the director of that agency to allow her to participate. We found her mother (no easy task) and convinced her to sign the authorization form. Together, we raised the funds she needed to go.

When the school year ended, she was notified that she had indeed been accepted to participate in the student foreign exchange program. She was given an assignment in Bogota, Columbia, where she became a part of a Columbian family for several months. When she returned, I realized the same whisper that Allie and I had heard on top of a mountain, Trina had heard in Bogota, "What else can I do that I never dreamed was possible?" Then toward the end of the following school year, Trina walked into my office. She had attended church the day before and had heard a man speak who was a representative with Teen Missions. Following his presentation, she had the opportunity to meet with him and ask him questions.

"Do you know they have never had group home kids go on any of their mission trips?" The despair from the previous year was absent. Instead, I saw a familiar smile. "Actually, Trina, I had never spent much time thinking about that. However, I am thinking we are about to start making a list and putting on our war paint, aren't we?" The truth was that she already had the list. This time, I smiled. She spent the entire next summer with Teen Missions in Australia. Trina went on to graduate from high school and then college. She also went on to marry and raise one son. Prior to going into the army, where she reported that she had a top-secret clearance and couldn't talk about what she did (and I believed her). She, together with her husband, became foster parents with us and modeled to multiple foster children how to climb walls that seek to block them in and rob them of any future. Together, they breathed hope to many who had come to them thinking of themselves as victims.

I had to smile.

MRS. G AND THE BLUE THING-A-MA-JIG

It had been a tradition for many years that on Christmas morning, the kids would all gather together in the large living room of the home and open Christmas presents. I realized the power and importance of traditions in bringing stability into the life of a child who had known trauma. However, I was also coming to understand that the process for how this tradition played out might need some attention.

For weeks prior to Christmas, several of the staff would spend an inordinate amount of time shopping for gifts. If you have children, you know the challenge of matching the right gift to the child, particularly gifts in your price range. Imagine shopping for a whole truckload of kids!

Once the gifts had been purchased, the staff would spend time wrapping them and making sure the correct labels were properly applied to each one. Finally, on Christmas morning, everyone would gather in the large living room, and one by one each gift would be handed out. Many times the children were excited to open the presents, but too often, there were several who were unhappy with what they got. It wasn't what they had imagined. Anticipation clashed with reality, and reality usually won. When I realized it was costing hundreds of dollars and many hours of staff time to purchase gifts for kids who may or may not appreciate them, it didn't make a whole lot of sense to me. I decided to change the process.

I gathered all the kids together and talked with them about Christmas. I asked them to write down on a sheet of paper a Christmas "wish list" of several items they would hope to receive for Christmas. They needed to include sizes, and colors where required. I then gathered up all the completed pages and had the lists put on individual cards. Each card would state the youth's first name, age, and list three of the items. I then wrote up a letter to go with each card that explained how I needed help with Christmas presents. "If you are reading this," it explained, "then you should also find a card attached. It would help us tremendously if you would select one of the items listed. Hopefully it is under $25. If you would purchase the item; wrap it; put a label on it with the child's name and the item you selected; and deliver it to the Home it would be sincerely appreciated by me and the kids."

I determined to spread the cards to anyone who would listen to me, and we would see what happened. If it didn't work, we could always go back to the old method. To be honest with you, I never really ever considered it wouldn't work. Instead, I was concerned some people in their generosity would buy everything on the list resulting in a few kids getting overloaded, and the others getting just a couple items. I thought I could deal with that type of problem.

It turned out as I had imagined. The word spread and numerous people called us or stopped by asking to take cards. As Christmas approached, instead of us having to spend time shopping for weeks and spending hundreds of scarce dollars on gifts, we were overrun with wrapped presents and people blessed for having the opportunity to help out in a genuine manner.

We had been doing it for several years when Florence came to me and asked for some guidance. Florence had served on the board and volunteered for over forty years. Now as a widow in retirement, with no children of her own, she continued to volunteer with projects for the kids regularly. To the kids, she was simply "Mrs. G." Florence had taken one of the cards and was very excited to spend the time shopping for the young lady, but she wasn't sure what it was the girl was requesting. "She wants a blue thing-a-ma-jig...I don't even know where to start looking." I didn't either. We laughed and she continued her search.

We decided to hold a Christmas Party on a Saturday morning about a week before Christmas and invite anyone who wanted to join us. That way, anyone who bought a present could be in the room when the gift was opened. Even if the person was giving the gift anonymously, they could be there and watch the excitement they had brought through their generosity.

We found the party to be so popular that the large living room was packed to overflowing with people. A group of volunteers would spend all morning helping our cook prepare a big luncheon for everyone immediately following the party. It was not uncommon for almost everyone to stay for the meal and linger long afterward. It was a great time.

> We found the party to be so popular that the large room was packed to overflowing with people.
> It was not uncommon for almost everyone to stay for the meal and linger long afterward.
> It was a great time.
> ...Usually!

...Usually! On this one particular year, when Florence had diligently hunted for the blue thing-a-ma-jig, the room was once again packed with kids, staff, and visitors. Florence came to me and with a big smile whispered..."I found it! It took a while, but I got it." She was so proud of herself. I had to laugh. What a wonderful woman!

The party started with a volunteer leading the room with some Christmas songs. I would follow by telling the Christmas story to everyone. Then several of the girls would do a skit or song. As they did, I would slip out of the room and put on my Christmas elf disguise. Santa was already waiting for me. When the skit was finished, a staff member would speak to the group, and before long, we could feel the walls shaking as we heard the call for "Sannn ta…Sannn ta…Sannn ta…Sannn ta." Eventually the door would slowly begin to open and in would walk Santa himself to cheers from the whole room. He would calm everyone down and begin talking to the quieted room until he decided it was time to hand out some gifts he had out in his sleigh. At that point, he would call loudly for his elf to start unloading the gifts.

Out in the hall a line of volunteers had all of the gifts for each child sitting in rows lining the hall and would take turns handing me one or two at a time. I would then shuffle into the room in my green suit with one or two gifts in my hands to give to Santa. I would tell him the child's name on the tag and point to her in the room, telling him where she was sitting. I realize many of us grew up thinking Santa was all knowing, but I learned he obviously was not. He had no idea who the kids were without my help. You can probably imagine the very first time I came shuffling into the room as an elf. The room went wild. I had never been accused of being too big, so there were some who thought the elf suit was appropriate. Most, however, saw the suit as being so out of character to the way I usually appeared as the CEO that they were genuinely and instantly surprised. Sometimes, we would have a girl in the room who had been in the program for over a year and had attended the previous year's party. She knew what was about to happen and often tried to tell the others. No one was sure to believe her or not…until the elf walked in…oh my!

Throughout the room, the girls were each sitting with a volunteer. It was the volunteer's job to write down the number and code on the tag of each gift along with a brief description of what the item was. Later, we would match up the codes with a master list giving us the names and addresses of each donor. The girls then wrote thank you notes to each. As I walked into the room carrying the gift containing what I knew was a blue thing-a-ma-jig, I handed it to Santa and let him know where she was seated. All over the room, kids were tearing paper off their gifts. Everyone seemed to be talking at once. No one was the center of attention for the whole room, except Santa. I watched as the young girl took the gift from Santa. I could see Florence sitting on a couch way across the room. She was sitting with another girl recording her items, but at this moment, I knew she was watching her labor of love be delivered. For that moment, nothing else seemed to be happening. As the girl carefully opened the gift, her smile lit up the whole room. From where I stood, I could not hear what she said, but I could see clearly as she reached into the box and pulled out the blue thing-a-ma-jig. Instantly her big smile turned to a scowl. She started speaking angrily to the volunteer sitting with her then she threw the gift on the floor.

> We are indeed created to give, but we also have been given the power to bless. We need to be careful we are not tricked into believing anything else.

In the early and mid-eighties, it was common for some girls and boys to be in care for several years and thus be very familiar with the traditions of the home. However, by the year 1990, we had shifted over to serving an all-girl population in our group homes who tended to stay for much shorter periods of time. It quickly became the norm for only one or two girls to have been present the year before. Many times, there were no girls present who had been in care the previous year. As I looked around the room, I realized that no one else seemed to be aware of what was going on. No one except Florence, who sat across the room frozen in place and me. I was speechless. The volunteer sitting with the girl said something to calm her then seemed to move on. Neither of them realized Florence and I were watching them. Before long, they had moved on to the next gift. The blue thing-a-ma-jig had become a memory. Afterward when I spoke with Florence, she was very gracious, but at the same time, I knew she had been wounded. I determined not to let that happen ever again if it was in my power to do so.

The next year early on the morning of the party, I called all the girls to the large living room where the party would be held. Most were still wrapped in their housecoats. I shared with them step by step how the day was going to play out. I talked about sitting on the floor so the guests could have the couches. I talked about how they needed to pair up with a volunteer so they could have a record of who to thank. I told them about how I had taken their wish lists and shared them with many people who had a desire to bless them. I did not tell them about the elf.

Then I shared with them the story of what had happened the previous year. As you can imagine, they were appalled that a girl would be so rude to Mrs. G. They all knew Mrs. G. I was careful to tell the story in such a manner that they would not be able to identify the girl involved and thus target her with their wrath.

At the time, she was still there, and yes, I had spoken with her about it in private. And it had become a genuine growing experience for her. I pointed out to them that the girl did not intend to hurt Mrs. G. In fact, she didn't even know she was. She didn't know the gift was from Mrs. G, as the tag simply said "From Santa." She also had no idea that Mrs. G and I were both watching her as she opened her gift. She got tricked. I asked if anyone could explain how she got tricked—silence. They weren't sure they understood.

I asked them how many gifts did any of the volunteers owe them. They all responded…"None." How many gifts does San Mar owe you…"None."

We talked about how it was true that none of them were owed any gifts at all. I asked them, "If someone doesn't owe you anything and end up not giving you anything, do you have a right to get upset?" They all demonstrated an amazing grasp of the obvious...

"No." They replied in unison.

"That's right, but there are those times when something happens that catches us by surprise. We see what others are getting and how much they are being blessed. We start thinking of all we want, and we start hoping that one of those wrapped boxes will have something we have been hoping for. It is not owed to us, but that doesn't stop us from still wanting things. It is understandable. Then when we open the box, and it is not just as we had imagined. Our emotions pull us down, or when the girl next to you has a pile of twelve gifts...big ones, and you only have three small ones. Doesn't it make you feel awful? Yet you have more than you were owed...but less than you hoped for."

A girl held the power in her hands to powerfully bless Mrs. G.
It was a reality that none of them had ever considered. The room was again silent. "You are in control. You just never knew control looked like this. Remember by your actions you can bless or destroy another person."

I reminded them that so often they feel like they are broken because everyone thinks of them as "group home girls." They're not as good as other kids. The room became eerily quiet as I spoke. Several nodded in agreement. I went on to tell them that Christmas was really about giving. The room was full of gifts because people wanted to give. They were blessed because of the generosity of all those people. I had often heard kids talk about how they felt bad because they could not give nice gifts to their own families. I suggested to them that they had been tricked into thinking they had nothing to give.

Once again, I saw a room filled with confused looks. I continued…"You all felt bad when I told you about Mrs. G. What if that girl would have been excited and loved what Mrs. G had given her? How do you think Mrs. G would have felt?"

They acknowledged that Mrs. G would have really felt good. That much was obvious to everyone.

Later that morning as Santa handed out the gifts, I watched between trips to the hallway as one girl opened a gift. It was a box containing the large makeup kit she had dreamed about. Carefully, she opened the gift and pulled out the makeup container. From where I stood across the room, I could see that one of the two doors on the front of it was broken. I stopped and watched. She smiled at the volunteer sitting with her and assured her that "Mr. A will make sure it gets exchanged for a nice one."

Good call! A second girl, a tiny twelve-year-old, opened a package and began screaming for joy as she announced to the whole room that she had got the blue jean skirt she had hoped for. She stood up and unwrapped it. As she began to unfold the skirt, it became obvious to all that the size was probably going to be baggy on a large very overweight Sumo wrestler used to wearing xxxx sizes. "It's…It's… It's…" She was wrapping it around her. "It's really big." She continued, "That's okay. They can exchange it for two!"

We are indeed created to give, but we also have been given the power to bless. We need to be careful we are not tricked into believing anything else.

PART 2

Taking Action

The only thing worse than being blind is having sight but no vision.
> —Helen Keller

The *journey to independence* that many youths are traveling doesn't come with a map and GPS coordinates and doesn't typically lead to a place called *happiness*. When things don't go as expected, it can be difficult to accept. When a youth has a history of trauma in their life, it can be even more difficult.

What follows are action steps for those on the *journey to independence* or for those seeking to understand a struggling youth and walk with them in a supportive manner. In many cases, these steps flow from observations made and lessons learned from hundreds of youth over many years and from my staff who have sought to respond in the most effective manner possible with a model of care that has worked.

THE INHERENT VALUE
OF EVERY INDIVIDUAL

For decades, I have listened to girls who have believed a message that they would be a person of worth when...they were prettier, taller, thinner, smarter, etc.

It is understandable. I have known many adults with a similar belief system. They simply filled in the blank differently...made more money, had more education, lost more weight, had the right friends, lived in the right neighborhood, drove the right car, etc...The message is the same; personal value is the result of personal efforts.

The problem I have observed over the years has been that once a person has achieved the goal that they expected would bring them to the point of personal worth, they often found that, in reality, they needed more money, more education, different friends, a better car, etc. Finding and retaining genuine personal worth in a material world that values only the best is very difficult, highly stressful, and rarely achievable.

In the book of Genesis (1:27), we are told that God created mankind in his own image. As I considered the implications of such a disclosure, I realized God has placed value in his creation, and that every person at the start of life begins with inherent value that has been given to them by their creator. Value wasn't withheld until a certain goal was met. It was given based on the character of God, not the accomplishment of the individual.

Were a person to accept that they had such value then it should subsequently influence everything they thought and did. What they did, or didn't do, would matter greatly.

If a person were brought up surrounded by a family and friends who recognized the inherent value of those around them as well as their own, it would be reasonable to expect that by the time a person reached adolescence they would have positive esteem, show evidence of a developing character, and even hope for the future.

However, if a person has been given a message from early childhood that any value they would ever know had to be earned then by adolescence, they may or may not be evidencing strength of character to others. It would really depend on how well they had managed to prove their value to the world and themselves.

Too often, many of the kids who were sent to us faced trauma in early childhood and as a result had an internal message that taunted them that they would never be of value. In some cases, they had even been surrounded by adults who had reinforced the message that there was no value in them and never would be. They were broken from the start so why even try. Such hopelessness was often reflected in their attitudes and behaviors.

Expecting a person who has received such messages over time to behave in a respectful manner may be optimistic as they have limited reference points. To withhold respect from them until such positive behaviors are exhibited is also not going to be helpful.

It is at this point that the adult who recognizes and accepts the reality of the inherent value of the individual needs to breathe hope to the hopeless.

How is this done? How does an adult strengthen their own understanding of the inherent worth they have themselves and subsequently communicate that message to the struggling youth? Here are a few action steps to get started on that path:

Action Steps

1. *Recognize and acknowledge that your own inherent value* is a daily living reality and not just a nice idea or a passing feeling. Someone making you feel unworthy does not change the truth. We live in a culture where the media continuously reinforces a message of earned value. Therefore, messages challenging inherent value will be normal and expected.

2. *Accept that no one can take away your God-Given inherent value* or the dignity that flows from that worth. For almost three decades, Nelson Mandela lived as a prisoner. He has been quoted as saying, "Any man or institution that tries to rob me of my dignity will lose." The reality of your inherent value is the foundation from which resiliency grows.

3. *Live with dignity.* The evidence that you recognize the value God has placed in you is seen in the dignity displayed in your words and actions. That being true, dignity builds character. Evidence of character growing within you is displayed as you seek to recognize and acknowledge the value and dignity of others on a daily basis. Live as if others are watching. They are.

4. *Reach beyond yourself and build up another.* When the pressure is on to earn or prove our value to ourselves and others, the focus is always on ourselves. When value is recognized as inherent, we have nothing to prove to anyone regarding our value as a person, including ourselves. The best way to turn such a statement into reality is to develop the practice of intentionally helping others with no thought of personal gain. In the process, make a point of reminding, or introducing the reality, of their own inherent worth to them.

5. *Develop an attitude and practice of self-compassion.* The concept of self-compassion is a result of the work of Dr. Kristen Neff. Her work is rooted in the idea that we all have inherent self-worth, and that one way to continue

to recognize this is to develop self-compassion, whereby you can develop a practice of applying grace to yourself. This limits unhealthy and often destructive self-criticism. Your expectations for yourself are often not reasonable or achievable. Developing self-compassion is to adopt a kind manner with yourself and to simply treat yourself the way you would treat a close friend. Self-compassion is not synonymous with letting yourself off the hook or not being accountable for your actions, but instead, it is a kind recognition of your pain, even your failure, with the goal of treating yourself with love and kindness so that you can more easily move forward, learn, and grow.[12]

6. *Surround yourself with a positive support network.* As noted previously, the reality of each person's inherent value is a foreign concept in American culture where earned value is the norm. In order to help move away from the destructive messages telling you to work harder for acceptance, a supportive network of others around you, who also embrace the truth of their value, is priceless. Such relationships need to be cultivated over time.

7. *Cultivate an attitude of gratitude.*[13] An attitude of gratitude means making it a habit to express thankfulness and appreciation in all parts of your life, on a regular basis, for both the big and small things alike. By making it a habit, we are developing a mindset that will help us during those periods where society's constant message of earned value is playing too loudly in our heads.

According to Lewis Howes in his new book, *The School of Greatness*, "If you concentrate on what you have, you'll always have more. If you concentrate on what you don't have, you'll never have enough."

---

[12] Kristen Neff, Self-compassion, (The proven power of being kind to yourself. 2015, June 23, New York, New York: William Morrow Paperbacks)

[13] J. Wong and J. Brown, How Gratitude Changes You and Your Brain. (Retrieved June 6, 2017 from http://greatergood.berkeley.edu/article/item/how_gratitude_changes_you_and_your_brain)

Paul Mills, a Professor of Family Medicine and Public Health at the University of California San Diego School of Medicine, conducted studies that looked at the role of gratitude on heart health. Among other things, he found that participants who kept a journal most days of the week, writing about two to three things they were grateful for (everything from appreciating their children to travel and good food), had reduced levels of inflammation and improved heart rhythm compared to people who did not write in a journal. And the journal-keepers also showed a decreased risk of heart disease after only two months of this new routine![14]

---

[14] Andrew Merle, The Blog: How to Have an Attitude of Gratitude, (Huffington Post, 2017, December 6)

PERSONAL OWNERSHIP
OF OUR LIVES

Over the years, there were approximately 2,500 youth in residence at San Mar in the various programs I operated. Many of them had been the victims of abuse. Sometimes the abuse had extended over a long period of time. I always found it interesting that two kids could come from the same home and similar abusive experiences yet react in very different ways. One would move forward, often against great odds, while the other remained a victim of their circumstances and the actions of others.

I came to realize that even worse than the actual physical and emotional abuse a child may have been freed from is a belief system that continues to hold them captive. It is a belief that lies to them and tells them that they will always be victims. They believe they are broken and always will be. It is not spoken. It is not always recognizable by others. It is not fixable, or so they believe. As a result, no one is coming to the rescue. There is no hope.

But...if there is inherent value in each individual then what they do, or do not do, matters. Since we are social beings living among others in community, then what we do, or do not do, has impact on those in our social context. We are subsequently accountable. We are responsible. We are interdependent.

Consider Genesis (chapters 2 and 3) once again and the account offered regarding Adam and his wife walking in the garden. God had said they were not to eat of the fruit on the tree of knowledge of good and evil. Everything else was theirs, including the forbidden fruit. They ate it.

Later, we learn that God asked them about what had happened.

Adam responded, "The woman you put here with me—she gave me some fruit from the tree, and I ate it."[15]

When God asked the woman to explain what happened she answered, "The serpent deceived me, and I ate." [16]

It appears as if denial and projection of responsibility and blame onto others is not new.

What would be the impact on our life if we were to believe that we had inherent value and act as if we had personal accountability for our words and actions without projecting responsibility onto others or blaming anyone?

Beginning today, you can make a choice to change and take complete ownership of your life. You can decide to take a new path and free yourself from the crippling mind-set that has been holding you back. Never again will you allow yourself the luxury of making excuses for why you cannot make progress. No longer will you indulge yourself with self-pity and the endless "poor me–isms." Blaming other people or outside events for your own misfortune are exercises not worthy of your consideration—your integrity is diminished, and your self-esteem will only suffer from these unproductive, time-wasting habits.

Tragedy is prevalent throughout our society. It's a sad fact of life that too many children grow up in abusive environments. Too often, otherwise perfectly normal people battle drug and gambling addictions or alcoholism. Poverty, hunger, and disease continue to be real chal-

---

[15] She wasn't named Eve until later.
[16] Genesis 3:12–13

lenges for millions of innocent people. In most cases, however, isn't it true that whatever your personal situation, there is someone else who is worse off than you? If the answer is yes, then doesn't it make sense to replace the thoughts of "woe is me" with thoughts of gratitude for the many blessings you do enjoy?

How is this done? How does a person who has developed habits of projecting, denying, and blaming others take ownership for their life?

Action Steps

1. *Accept the reality of your own inherent value.* If you have value, then what you do or don't do matters. It is difficult to accept ownership if you have a belief that denies any worth you may have. Make sure your belief systems are providing you with the proper foundation for you to build upon.

2. *Forgive yourself and others.* We have all fallen short of perfection multiple times. Forgiveness is the reality of letting go of that wrong committed against you, or someone you care about, by someone else or even by yourself. Forgiveness is a willingness to let go of the negative feelings associated with the wrong. Forgiveness is a conscious act of volition made by a free will. The associated feelings flow from your belief system. To be a person who takes ownership for your actions, you must begin with those areas of unforgiveness where you are held captive. Forgiveness of yourself and others enables you to move forward with a clear conscience taking genuine ownership of your actions. If forgiving yourself or someone else seems impossible to you, it may be because it must be accomplished through the superhuman grace of God. Ask for it as God desires to provide grace and forgiveness to those who sincerely stand in need.

Where you have genuinely wronged others and are willing to admit it and own it go to them and seek to make it right. Note that saying you are sorry does not require the other person to even acknowledge your presence. However, when you own your actions and admit to having done something that requires forgiveness, you're asking for a response. Whether or not the other person actually forgives you is not a determination as to when, or if, to seek forgiveness. It is also recognized that forgiveness is a superhuman act and requires the grace of a forgiving God. It is also important that when you ask for forgiveness, it should be sincere and evidenced in action. For example, there may be restitution needed to make the wrong done right.

3. *Watch your self-talk.* Take note of the things you are constantly telling yourself. Your self-talk is a primary factor in your ability to overcome any major challenge. If you are constantly telling yourself that you aren't good enough or that you aren't smart enough or attractive enough, it should not surprise you when you continually sabotage yourself in relationships and other areas of your life. Where your words are destructive toward yourself and others, change them. Develop language that builds up and strengthens both yourself and those around you. If you are not clear as to whether or not your self-talk is destructive, ask a close friend to provide you with some honest feedback. Then be willing to humbly listen.

4. *Accept responsibility appropriately and act.* Taking ownership is more than simply accepting your situation or taking responsibility for the decisions that have brought you to this place in your life. Taking ownership also means that you are committed to taking action toward resolving the challenges that you've identified as barriers to your personal success. Taking action may involve getting help from a doctor, pastor, friend, or anyone who has the knowledge and skills to guide you toward a path of personal ownership and

recognition of your inherent worth as a person created in the image of a personal God.

5. *Make your bed.*[17] Navy Seal William H. McCraven, commander of the forces that led the raid to kill Osama bin Laden, in his 2014 commencement speech at the University of Texas advised graduates, "If you want to change the world, start off by making your bed. If you make your bed every morning, you will have accomplished the first task of the day. It will give you a small sense of pride, and it will encourage you to do another task, and another, and another. And by the end of the day that one task completed will have turned into many tasks completed." Gretchen Rubin, best-selling author and happiness researcher, says "When I was researching my book on happiness, this was the number one most impactful change that people brought up over and over."[18] Establish the routine of discipline.

6. *Choose to grow.* Whereas we are created in the image of a perfect God, we are not perfect ourselves. We will fail. When we do, we have the choice to give up and feel sorry for ourselves, or we can choose to grow and learn from our mistakes. At 5'4", God has positioned me to look most of the kids I have worked with in the eyes. However, one young girl upon our first encounter asked me, "How tall are you?" To which I told her, "Six foot, four." Being very observant she commented, "You can't be an inch over six foot tall!" I explained that if we fail but learn from our failures, we can grow. I had failed enough times but learned from the experiences so many times that I had to be at least six foot four. I believe she missed my point completely. I trust you will not.

[17] Andrew Merle, The Blog: Make You Bed, Change Your Life, (Huffington Post, 2015, August 24)
[18] Gretchin Rubin, The Happiness Project, (2015, Harper)

VISION AND HOPE

Vision: The act of imagining what could be in such a manner that it courageously opens the door to the future and calls for action.

For many years, I organized a four-day bicycle tour of the C & O Canal. The Canal, is a 184.5-mile-long trail that runs from Cumberland in Western Maryland to Georgetown in Washington. It is a national park.

The first two nights of the adventure, the participants would stay in campgrounds near the trail. On the third night, there were no campgrounds near the trail, so I would arrange for the entire group of a hundred or more participants to stay in a hotel in the area. When we did, all of the costs were covered through sponsors of the event.

Months in advance of the tour, I would begin the process of trying to find a hotel interested in hosting our entire group for a price we could afford on our limited budget.

Eventually, I would find a hotel where the management appeared to want our business and would contract for us to stay with them.

I began to notice that as the date got closer, I would often get a call or an e-mail regarding changes they were needing to make to the contract. Sometimes I would agree to the changes, and sometimes I would not.

As the pattern continued, I realized that when I made the reservation, there were very few other reservations scheduled for the night we were planning to be there. The hotel didn't want to turn away many paying customers even if it was for a discounted rate, so they would contract with us. However, as the date drew closer, they would inevitably begin to fill up. Occasionally, a hotel would get to the point where they were having to turn away customers from whom they would be getting a much higher rate. On one particular occasion, I noticed what seemed to be resentment from the management as we were continuously having to address problems that arose. I realized I had been able to convince some to give us great rates, but I had not imparted to them a passion for our mission. They were giving a discount to meet their needs, and if it helped us, it was secondary to fulfilling their mission.

People do things for their reasons. When I think they are doing things for my reasons, without first having caught a vision that moves them to action, I am mistaken, and they are often resentful or indifferent to what I think is important when things don't go as they envisioned. It was a lesson I would remember.

Many years later, we began a work in the Bester community of Hagerstown. We had opened an office near the local elementary school and had begun developing a partnership with several local organizations, including the local school.

As we met with the teachers, they identified to us that one of the greatest problems they faced in the school was poor attendance. They noted that their school had been identified as having the worst attendance problem of any school in the county.

We realized that poor attendance in elementary school impacts many other factors including high school graduation rates and even employment later in life. We began trying to understand what was underlying the attendance problem.

The teachers believed there were several factors contributing to the high absenteeism, but the greatest common reason given was related to health issues. As we discussed it, the teachers expressed their belief that the presence of a health clinic at the school would go far to address this concern.

We began to study the issue in depth and realized there seemed to be some validity to their observation. We had no idea how to start or run a health clinic but targeted the development and operation of a health clinic in the school as one of our main goals for the year. We knew that for this to occur, we were going to have to partner with others who had greater expertise than we did.

Based on the lesson learned years earlier, that people do things for their reasons and never for mine, we determined that in order for us to have any success whatsoever in the community, we would need first of all to build a network of believers. That is, we would need to find a core group of people who understood and embraced a vision for seeing the community transformed.

I tried several times to schedule a meeting with the administrators at the local hospital but kept being turned down. Eventually, I was able to develop a strong connection with the director of the Community Free Clinic, who thought our plan to go into the local elementary school was exciting. They were located only one block from the school and looked forward to seeing how it was going to work out. Robin, the director, explained that they only worked with adults, but they really hoped we were successful with the kids.

I asked Robin if they didn't work with kids, or if they wouldn't work with kids. She looked at me for a moment then laughed. She agreed that they had not worked with kids up to that point due to several obstacles preventing them from doing so. She agreed to work together with us to see if the obstacles could be removed.

As we moved forward, I noticed that Robin was using many physicians in her clinic who worked at the hospital. I asked her if she had some strong connections with the administration. She did.

She agreed to set up a meeting with three of the hospital's top administrators and the two of us.

As we gathered in the conference room at the hospital, I began by thanking them for the opportunity to meet together.

Almost immediately the Chief Operations Officer interrupted, "Stop…What is it that you are asking us to do?"

It was a fair and reasonable question. It was even expected. It was my answer that wasn't expected.

"I'm not asking you for anything."

Looks of confusion appeared instantly on the faces of the three administrators sitting in front of me.

"Then why are we here?"

Once again the question was both reasonable and expected. I explained, "If I give you a list of needs, you will give me a list of valid reasons why it can't happen. I already know what the obstacles are and why it can't happen. All I hope to do is share a vision with you in the time I have. If you catch that vision and believe what I share is possible, then you will tell me how you can be a part of it. If you see no merit in what I share, then I will thank you for your time and move on."

"Go ahead."

I did, and for the next hour, I shared how a health clinic at the elementary school in the Bester community would strengthen their commitment to be a community hospital.

For quite a while, we had believed what we were doing with youth in our care was both meaningful and effective. In April 2005, the

Baltimore Sun had run a week-long series on residential care in Maryland and had identified numerous areas of concern. However, they also featured us on the front page of their April thirteenth edition in which investigative reporter, Jon Rockoff, identified us as operating a model program.

We had seen the transforming power that a genuinely caring adult connecting with a youth in healthy ways could unleash. We had experienced the impact that resulted when an entire team of like-minded adults worked together to value a youth.

By 2013, we had begun asking if we should begin thinking differently as to how we could have a greater impact. As we struggled with strategic questions regarding increasing the effectiveness of what we were doing, we began asking what impact we might have if we began working with families who were struggling before their problems had risen to the point where their children had to be removed. We had developed an effective model that responded after the family had experienced crisis and often trauma. What would happen if we shifted to include a prevention model? As we wrestled with moving forward, we resolved to be child centered, family focused, and community engaged.

As I sat with the hospital administrators, I explained how we had opened an office in the Bester community and had begun working with the school. I shared how Casey Family Programs, a national foundation dedicated to the welfare of children, had chosen to partner with us. I explained how the Fletcher Foundation had made one of their largest contributions ever to support the work we were doing.

Then I shared the obstacles that the teachers saw and how they identified the need for a health clinic in the school. Robin shared how they were working to position themselves to be able to address this community need.

At that point, the CFO looked at the other two and explained to them that if they made a few changes here and an adjustment there, he thought they would be able to provide some help. In response, the director of development, one of the three hospital administrators in the meeting, started laughing causing everyone in the room to stop. She went on to explain that I was right. They were catching the vision and instead of seeing barriers they were trying to figure out how to create pathways around the obstacles.

The clinic became a reality. Within two years, the Washington County Board of Education recognized the Bester Elementary School with the award for having the Most Improved Attendance of any school in the county.

Whether forming a healthy connection with one youth or connecting with multiple others so as to impact an entire community, it all begins with a clear vision of what can be. Vision inspires forward motion.

Action Steps to Develop a Vision Plan

What could you do if there were nothing holding you back? We would have started a health clinic. Trina would have gone to a foreign country as part of a student exchange program. Clarify your vision based on what is needed, not on what you think is possible and attainable.

1. Write down your vision with timelines.
2. Identify the actual and the perceived obstacles to you being able to turn your vision into reality.
3. Share your vision to create a network of believers who will join you in seeing the obstacles knocked down and the vision become reality.
4. Identify specific tasks to be completed and invite believers in your growing network to join you in carrying them out.

5. Cultivate an attitude of gratitude daily so as to enable you to get back up and keep going after you get knocked down from running into a wall.
6. Keep building your believer network and getting back up. Celebrate even small successes with your network to help everyone stay focused.
7. When your vision is fulfilled, start the process all over again.

AUTHENTIC TRUST

Trust is an option and choice. It is developed over time but can be destroyed in an instance. It is important that we live our lives in such a manner that we are demonstrating trust in all areas. We never know who may be watching.

On the fourth Saturday morning of every month for many years, we would hold a meeting of our volunteer association. These meetings would involve numerous volunteers putting on a program for the girls in all our programs. Every month would be something different. Meetings tended to be fun and usually somewhat educational. On one particular morning, we were just finishing up the meeting when a man entered the front foyer and asked for me. Within moments, a volunteer led him into the large room where I was. It was Gary. I had known him for several years and had ridden bikes with him many times. He was a strong and experienced rider who had often pushed me to my limits. I noticed he was carrying a canvas pouch in his hand. It looked important. Everyone was instantly curious as he walked over and shook my hand announcing, as he did, he had a problem. Whereas, we were off to the side of the room, I realized everyone had suddenly gone silent, and I wondered if I should invite him into the hallway. All eyes were on Gary and his mysterious canvas pouch.

He didn't give me a chance as he started explaining. He had just driven around the bend in the road. Everyone knew exactly the bend he was talking about. It was less than a mile away. Numerous accidents occurred there on a regular basis. I began imagining an accident had just occurred, and he needed help. It would not be the first time I had been asked to respond to an accident there. He continued explaining that when he went around the bend, he saw a big canvas bag sitting in the road. It looked important and obviously out of place, so he pulled over and grabbed it before it got hit and whatever was in it ruined. He held up the gray bag.

When he opened the bag standing there in the road, he was shocked at what he found.

He was obviously shaken and stopped at that point to open the bag to show me.

I stepped forward to stop him, fearful that what was in that bag could trigger some of the kids in the room who had known severe trauma. When I did, he realized my concern and smiled.

"No…don't worry. I came here immediately because I trust you." He opened the bag. It was filled with money…large bills. Lots of them.

"I didn't know what to do. I knew you would know how to handle this."

To my amazement, the room was still silent, but there were a lot of very big eyes staring at that bag. I realized everyone was waiting to see what I was going to do. I also realized that my character had been on display with Gary and everyone in the room for a long time. I had never framed it as such, but apparently they had.

"How much is in the bag, Gary?" I asked.

He didn't know and hadn't touched it. I opened the bag, hoping there were no exploding dye canisters in it. There weren't.

There was a checkbook with a name. I went into the office and pulled out a phone book. I found the name listed and called.

There was no answer, but I did get an answering machine. I left a message. Needless to say, I got a call back pretty quickly. The man lived several miles away. He had gone out to his car earlier that morning and had set the canvas bag on the roof as he carefully opened the car door. He was so focused on not spilling his coffee as he carefully opened the door and slid into the car that he forgot the bag sitting on top of the roof. He was on his way to his office but was going to go by the bank and make a deposit. I had assumed it was for his business. He didn't say, and I didn't ask. It had remained on the roof for several miles until he went around the sharp bend. Gary must have been coming along right afterward. However, the bag wasn't missed until he arrived at the bank and realized what he had done. As panic set in, he immediately retraced his path, but by that time, the bag was nowhere to be found. He entered his house in near panic and found my message waiting for him. We were able to reunite him with his missing bag and money. I did ask him to count it while we were together, which he did. It was all there. I never did ask him how much it was.

It was a lesson to me on the importance of living our lives with integrity consistently as we never know when we are going to be put on display. I also recognized and acknowledged the real character on display was shown by Gary as he acted in a responsible manner when no one was watching. Trust often grows in silence without applause or recognition, but its touch is powerful.

The girls all expected me to return the money, but they also recognized that Gary could have walked away with all the money, and no one would have known. It opened the door for some interesting discussion. Several of the girls commented how they would have liked to have the money and would have kept it. Yet they also acknowledged how they needed to have people in their lives who they could trust. They also realized the desire and need to be trustworthy themselves. Initially, one girl was insisting that she could be trustworthy to her friends but still take advantage of the opportunity presented if she found a bag of money. As she talked, it became clear that she really would have reservations about trusting someone whose trust could be bought or was situational. It was also clear that few have had strong role models demonstrating to them the power of trust lived out in a life. It was a lesson they would remember long afterward.

Action Steps

1. *Give more than you expect to have given to you.* The enemies of trust are cynicism, self- centeredness, and indifference where one expects more than they are willing to give.

2. *Genuine trust can never be taken for granted but must be continuously cultivated through commitments and truth.* Trust and truth go together. Lying is always a breach of trust. True leadership must be based on trust. The first step in addressing distrust is to openly talk about it.

3. *Foster Creativity.* The essential virtue of trust is its openness—its celebration of possibilities. Most damaging, but nearly invisible, aspect of a culture of control is the loss of creativity. The seeds of distrust are prevalent. To trust is to open new doors and to seize opportunities.

4. *Develop the skill of listening to others and regularly express genuine appreciation for the perspective and contribution of others.* The strength of a trust culture is the ability to (recognition of the need to) appreciate the perspective of others. Coming to the point of understanding, the perspective of another is much more important than airing one's affections and grievances. Trust is a social practice. Trust is both earned as well as given and must be built through consistent routines and practices. For those who have not known trauma, trust is often an invisible medium that is assumed. When needs go unmet, the child naturally becomes distrustful. When abuse is introduced, they grow with an inordinate suspicion of others. Speak words of encouragement that sow seeds of trust.

5. *Expect risk but learn to think in terms of opportunities.* Genuine trust always involves risk. However, you must learn to think of trust in terms of positives and pathways to seizing the opportunities available. The tendency is to typically think in terms of risks and vulnerabilities, which lead to no forward motion.

6. *Take ownership of your life and actions* so that you live with integrity and others are able to trust you without great risk. Show people you care about them. When people know you care about their interests as much as your own, they will trust you. If they believe you are out for yourself, you become a risk, and they will say to themselves, "Watch out for that person."

7. *Create and maintain a culture of trust.* Begin by defining your core values and develop understandings as to how they are lived out.

CONSISTENCY

Living without Contradictions

For years, we trained all of our staff who worked directly with the girls in the group homes regarding the importance of establishing and maintaining consistency in what they do. It was often a topic in staff meetings usually because some inconsistencies in routine had resulted in some negative outcomes or simply mixed messages and confusion. However, it wasn't until I spent time with my sons as they walked Roo and Shey around a lake in California that I saw the power of consistency in action.

Dan, my youngest son and the experienced dog trainer, had explained how the most challenging aspect of training a dog was his being able to get through to the owner regarding the importance of being consistent in doing the right things over time.

As we walked, Roo would walk by Dan's side until Dan would quietly signal her. At that point, she would run and play. Eventually, Dan would signal from a distance. At that moment, Roo would run to Dan's side. At the same time, my oldest son, Kit, was walking Shey. Throughout the walks, Shey would tug at his leash as Kit would seek to keep him under his control. I noted that Kit and Shey both appeared somewhat frustrated with the experience.

I realized Kit had watched Dan train many dogs and had listened to him explain how it was done but was undoubtedly thinking that Dan had never trained Shey. It was obvious Shey needed a different type of intervention to address his high energy level and independence. Shey was clearly a good-natured dog with no indication of a mean or rebellious spirit in him at all. He was simply distracted by everything around him...constantly. When that happened, Kit, as the trainer, became invisible.

Dan must have sensed the frustration as he encouraged Kit to continue doing what he was doing. Kit later told me that in less than two weeks, Shey was walking around the lake by his side without the leash. Kit's consistency in training had helped Shey bring his behavior under control.

By definition, consistency is mostly referred to as adherence to the same principles in a steadfast way without contradiction. Consistency is the key to success; not only in training dogs or working with challenging youth, but in all you are doing.

Since consistency is by definition developing the habits of applying the same things repeatedly without deviation or contradiction, instead of action steps as to how to develop consistency, it is more important to grasp the true value of having the right practices applied consistently.

The Value of Consistency

1. *Consistency allows for measurement.* In order for you to know if what you are doing in any given area is effective, you will need to measure the change that has occurred over a period of time. Consistency establishes defined boundaries that can provide points by which progress can be measured. For example, Dan had observed that he was able to train a dog to walk next to a handler without a leash in

five twenty-minute sessions if the handler was consistent in applying the instructions. If the handler was not consistent and gave into frustrations, the training was delayed, or in some cases, never completed.

2. *Consistency creates accountability.* Just as dignity is the manifestation of inherent worth in the life of an individual who recognizes their value, accountability results from a framework of consistency. Accountability is the opportunity presented to an individual to grow as a result of feedback and support offered through a social network of which they are a participating member. Consistency in our programs with the youth afforded them the opportunity to know what was expected of them at any given point and what was needed to be successful.

3. *Consistency establishes trust.* Trust is born from repeated actions that demonstrate a clear message of integrity, safety, and reliability. Trust can never be purchased but is realized over time through consistent actions. No relationship can grow and continue without consistency over time. For a person who has experienced trauma through abuse, particularly when such abuse has been over an extended period of time, establishing routines and healthy patterns become one of the steps in the healing process. Healthy consistency in the parenting of young children is also instrumental in building a foundation of trust from the start.

4. *Consistency breeds credibility.* If you want to be taken seriously, be consistent. Youth need a predictable flow of information from you. Kids pay as much or more attention to what you do as to what you say. Consistency in your leadership serves as a model for how they will behave. If you fail to follow through with what you say, all credibility is gone.

5. *Consistency establishes and reinforces your mission/message.* When something doesn't work, I look back at what happened and ask some serious questions. Did we shift gears too quickly? Did part of the team not deliver on a com-

mitment? Or was the expected outcome off base from the start? Usually, the reason tracks back to lack of consistency.

6. *Consistent action becomes a habit and can be learned and developed.* Small disciplines repeated with consistency lead to great achievements accomplished over time. By establishing consistent routines, it helps you to overcome those periods where your feelings demand you take the day off. The person who takes action every single day toward the attainment of their goal will always triumph over those who do it every once in a while. Desire is not enough. A person waiting for inspiration limits achievement to times when conditions are desirable. And conditions are rarely always desirable. Creating healthy rituals will take you further than desires and passions.

7. *Consistency creates momentum and fosters sustainability.* Surprisingly, doing something every day or nearly every day is actually far easier to sustain than doing it once in a while. Consistency is more about sustainability than it is about speed.

EPILOGUE

To finish the moment, to find the journey's end in every step of
the road, to live the greatest number of good hours, is wisdom.
—Ralph Waldo Emerson

I started by sharing my adventure of riding my bicycle from Snowmass to Independence Pass in Colorado. For several years, I had wondered if climbing such a mountain on a bicycle was possible for me to do. Once I committed to finding out, I spent months in preparation for the climb. When the day arrived, I spent hours actually climbing the mountain. Yet when I arrived at the top, I only spent a few minutes there.

Simply being at the destination was never the goal, or I could have done as several others had and chosen to ride up the mountain in a school bus that was available to those who didn't want to ride their bikes thirty miles, in thinning air, to the summit. Completion of the journey itself, on a bicycle as evidenced by standing at the summit, was the goal.

For many of the youth I have known, their focus has been firmly on being, and remaining, at the destination of "independence." Over time, I came to realize that the desire to arrive and remain at the perceived destination was due to the belief that the destination was actually the land of happiness where adults no longer wielded the power and authority to tell them what to do. It was the land where they would make all their own decisions. In reality, it was a land of make-believe and fantasy.

In 2012, I traveled to Peru and hiked the Inca Trail into the mountain kingdom of Machu Picchu, one of the seven wonders of the world. It is believed Machu Picchu was a royal estate built for the Inca king Pachacutec around AD 1450.

The ruins of Machu Picchu sit atop a high mountain surrounded by thick jungle. At the base of the mountain is the village of Aguas Calientes. From the village, there is a roadway that zig zags up the mountain to the stone city. Today there are buses running throughout the day carrying tourists from the train station in Aguas Calientes up the mountain.

However, the guides tell the story from ancient times when the city could only be entered by those who had come by way of walking the Inca Trail. That trail, running about thirty-five miles, extended over three difficult mountain peaks, one of which was just under 14,000 feet. The path itself had been hand crafted from thousands of stones cut from granite and fitted together in an intricate display of masterful engineering. It took four days to hike to the city along the trail. (At least it took me four days. The Incas no doubt did it quicker.)

The king had observed that those entering the city who had walked the challenging trail had been so changed by the experience that it caused them to see life in a different manner than those who had not walked the path. Therefore, he decreed only those who entered by the more challenging route could pass through the gates of his city. Everyone else was forbidden under threat of their life.

I hiked the trail in the thin air and saw amazing wonders. If I would have arrived, after four days of very challenging hiking, and found there really was no city of Machu Picchu, I would have still had the memories of the amazing stonework that extended for miles; llamas running wild at 13,000 feet and eating out of my hand; two hundred varieties of orchids displaying their beauty; standing by ancient ruins and looking down onto the clouds; multiple ruins from an obviously proud and educated people; local porters laden with enormous loads on their backs and wearing sandals; and beautiful and steep mountains unique to only that part of the world. It would not have been a wasted journey.

To the youth on a journey to *happiness*, who one day faces the reality that there really is no such village, city, state, or nation where they can live completely self-centered and happy, the information is difficult to accept causing many continual struggle for years. However, to those youths who had the opportunity to form a healthy connection with a genuinely caring adult as they journeyed through adolescence, the reality that there is no kingdom waiting may help them to remember and recognize lessons from their journey. Such as: taking personal ownership of their lives, or recognizing and claiming the inherent value they have, or finding the courage to accept the challenge to step out and do things they never dreamed possible. It need not be a journey wasted. They may even continue their journey and find happiness and fulfillment waiting for them in the realm of interdependence.

If you are the adult who has sought to value and connect with a struggling youth and breathe hope into their lives, don't give up. Remember the brain continues to develop until the early to mid-twenties. As it does, the context you have provided for all the pieces of their lives fitting together into a meaningful whole will make more and more sense to them. Not only is that youth a person of extreme worth and value, so are you. What you do matters!

About the Author

Bruce T. Anderson, MSSW, LCSW

For 33 years Bruce served as the CEO of San Mar, a nationally accredited nonprofit organization in Western Maryland providing residential care to adolescent girls, treatment foster care to girls and boys of all ages and community mental health services. He is a graduate of Taylor University and the University of Cincinnati. Bruce continues to maintain an active schedule of telling his stories in speaking and training events and adding more cycling and hiking adventures to the long list of adventures already completed. He lives in Western Maryland.

CPSIA information can be obtained
at www.ICGtesting.com
Printed in the USA
FFHW022047190819
54349627-60049FF